CHILDREN OF POVERTY

STUDIES ON THE EFFECTS
OF SINGLE PARENTHOOD,
THE FEMINIZATION OF POVERTY,
AND HOMELESSNESS

edited by

STUART BRUCHEY
ALLAN NEVINS PROFESSOR EMERITUS
COLUMBIA UNIVERSITY

A GARLAND SERIES

TEACHERS' ATTITUDES TOWARD CHILDREN OF DRUG-RELATED BIRTHS

LADY JUNE HUBBARD

GARLAND PUBLISHING, Inc.
A MEMBER OF THE TAYLOR & FRANCIS GROUP
NEW YORK & LONDON / 1998

Library of Congress Cataloging-in-Publication Data

Hubbard, Lady June.
    Teachers' attitudes toward children of drug-related births /
Lady June Hubbard.
        p.   cm. — (Children of poverty)
    Includes bibliographical references and index.
    ISBN 0-8153-3182-7 (alk. paper)
    1. Children of pre-natal substance abuse—Education—United
States. 2. Children of pre-natal substance abuse—United States—
Social conditions. 3. Teachers—United States—Attitudes.
4. Special education teachers—United States—Attitudes. I. Title.
II. Series.
LC4806.4.H83 1998
371.91—dc21
                                                                98-25633

Printed on acid-free, 250-year-life paper
Manufactured in the United States of America

Contents

List of Tables

List of Figures

Preface

The author acknowledges and applauds a continued research agenda on children exposed prenatally to cocaine and the developmental effects on the child . The more recent studies continue to investigate and report on the more positive outcomes of cocaine exposed school-aged children (Richardson, Conroy & Day, 1996; Hurt et al., 1997). Many of these children are the offspring of drug abusing mothers who self-report to what is described as light use. How our children of heavy, chronic users may fare, requires futher investigation. As Frank and Zuckerman (1993) so poignantly emphasize, we do not want to further stigmatize these children or their mothers. As researchers and educators though, we must responsibly continue to investigate and report accurate and relevant information and findings. This includes the need to underscore the issues surrounding toxicity and potency of crack-cocaine ingestion by the user throughout the literature (Zuckerman & Frank, 1994). It also suggests distinguishing between studies of cocaine in its powder form, and developing methods for examining the impact of cocaine in it's most toxic form - crack.

Acknowledgments

I give thanks to the Creator and all who assisted me spiritually, professionally and personally with this endeavor. I especially want to thank my brother Jawanza for his endless support and commentary, and Detris for her untiring support and suggestions. To my elders, those past and present I give credit for their examples of perseverance, insight and scholarship.

I wish to acknowledge the foundational assistance and support Dr. Penny Hauser-Cram. She has offered so much to me in terms of time, scholarly inquiry, and professional mentoring and growth. I also thank Dr. Ron Nuttall, and Dr. Thomas Bidell, for their helpful suggestions, direction and support. A special thank you to Dr. Nuttall, who encouraged me with endless hours of support to pursue this topic and methodology from the beginning. A warm thank you to Dr. Bidell and Dr. Adams for their moral support.

I wish to acknowledge the contributions of the respondents for their assistance with this investigation, and hopefully their contribution to a greater understanding and growing body of literature on issues of drug-related births.

Introduction

Children of drug-related births in the U.S. are presently entering into our schools in increasing numbers and we cannot wait until they are grown to provide assistance for them. This book examines teachers' attitudes toward children of crack/cocaine-exposed births and teachers' expectations of these students' social and neurobehavioral responses. There is a need to explore the subtle racial and socio-economic biases that may impact the attitude of those designated to help these children. The perceptions and attitudes of everyone involved is a clear and present concern. From the first day these children enter an educational institution, their reception by the adults and their peers is of prime importance. Since there is no one profile of the crack/cocaine exposed child, just as with other children, each child will have unique needs. Some of them will have special needs, many of which are not presently understood by the masses of educators, counselors or administrators.

As a member of our society, the influences on any individual's perceptions are varied and many. Teachers have been inundated with a barrage of media portrayals, rumors and misinformation about these children and their ability to perform in an academic environment. Many drug-exposed children have defied the stigmas generated by the media, as will many more.

Educators have a critical role in their interrelationships with students within the educational environment. Modification to their approach to the drug-exposed population may be necessary to promote a maximum level of success for each child. Teachers have a varied educational background around issues and outcomes of drug use and abuse. Some have had extensive exposure, while others have no prior training, or only a minimal understanding of these issues.

Many special needs teachers are familiar with some of the developmental difficulties drug-exposed children may face, and yet not be clear in their approach. Developing an understanding and refinement of the classroom teacher is imperative to the success of the drug-exposed child. Their level of success and the educational context are interdependent.

There is a need for the dissemination of more drug information and it is our responsibility to provide that information to the educators. It is also the responsibility of educators to collaborate and collectively assist these children in progressing through the educational system.

Teachers' Attitudes toward Children of Drug-Related Births

CHAPTER I

Background

Between 1992 and 1993, the use of illicit drugs by individuals in the United States has increased by one million to 12 million, out of a survey population of 207 million (Office of National Drug Control Policy, 1996). The number of people who reported ingestion of cocaine within the thirty days prior to the survey was 1.9 million. Drug use by women and young adults is increasingly disproportionate to that of other groups. Lifetime use by the childbearing age group (26-34 yrs) had doubled, and was higher in contrast to any other age group (Household Survey on Drug Abuse, 1993; Office of National Drug Control Policy, 1996; Gold, 1993).

In 1989 the National Association for Perinatal Addiction Research and Education (NAPARE) estimated that 375,000 newborns each year would incur serious health hazards due to prenatal drug use by their pregnant mothers (Barton, Harrigan & Tse, 1995; Chasnoff, 1992; Pinkerton, 1991). In a 1992 survey of women delivering live births, it was reported that over one million infants were born with prenatal exposure to drugs (National Pregnancy & Health Survey, 1996).

STATEMENT OF THE PROBLEM

As the number of drug-related births increases, so does the entry of these children into the educational system. Although the numbers of these births are already high, it is anticipated that these estimates will continue to increase (Office of National Drug Control Policy, 1996). Lumsden (1990) notes that it has been predicted that within a few years, 40-60 percent of inner-city students will be either drug-related births or children born to substance abusers.

Children who exhibited some level of crack/cocaine in their system at birth are the focus of this investigation. For these children, problems in the educational system may begin with or be exacerbated by the attitudes of school personnel, particularly classroom teachers. This study was designed to investigate teachers' attitudes toward children who were cocaine-exposed at birth. The study also examines the influence of educational training on the resultant attitudes toward drug-exposed children.

The growing body of literature indicates an increased awareness and speculation of the possible damage prenatal drug use may cause, and the heightened concern over subsequent malformations or developmental disabilities in the newborn. Crack cocaine is a smokeable freebase form of cocaine which is fifteen to twenty times more potent than powder cocaine (Cook, Peterson, & Moore, 1990). Once ingested, cocaine has an almost instantaneous euphoric effect on the user (Rist, 1990). Drugs that are inhaled or injected by pregnant women, such as crack/cocaine, cross the placenta more rapidly than drugs taken orally (Cook, Peterson & Moore, 1990). Cocaine is also highly fat soluble and passes with ease across the placenta (Weiss, Mirin & Bartel, 1994). The developing fetus metabolizes and excretes drugs that cross the placental barrier at a much slower rate than the mother (Chasnoff, 1992; Cook, Peterson & Moore). The drugs therefore stay in the system of the fetus longer where their effect is often aggravated by it's small size.

The deleterious effects of general drug use on the fetus is well documented in the literature. The specific independent effects of cocaine, however, are less well-known because many newborns referred to as "cocaine-exposed" have been exposed to multiple deleterious factors, such as maternal polydrug use (Chasnoff, 1989; Kaye, Elkind, Goldberg & Tytun, 1989; Richardson & Day, 1994; Snodgrass, 1994; Tronick, 1991; Weiss, Mirin & Bartel, 1994) and have had poor environmental supports due to poverty, inadequate nutrition, and infectious disease (Weiss, Mirin & Bartel, 1994; Vincent, 1991; Zuckerman, Frank & Brown, 1995). Zuckerman (1991) posits that complications arise around the identification of the effects of cocaine as a single chemical of abuse because, in practice, the abuse is rarely limited to only one drug.

Legal drugs often affect the developing fetus, although not as severely. For example, the use of caffeine (e.g., cola drinks and coffee) and over-the-counter drugs (e.g., cough syrup and cigarettes) by a pregnant mother may cause fetal distress. Such drugs are often abused and may not come to the forefront in the selection of exposed or control groups. Medical use of many psychotherapeutics by pregnant women has exceeded one-half of a million (National Pregnancy and Health Survey, 1996).

Early research indicates that cocaine-exposed infants suffer abnormal nervous system development, impaired motor skills/reflexes, seizures, and unusual electrical brain activity (Gold, 1993; Office of Technology Assessment, 1990; Weiss, Mirin & Bartel, 1994). Prenatal trauma to the nervous system appears to result in a range of developmental difficulties, including poor health, behavioral deviations, and structural anomalies. As the children approach school age, researchers are able to identify problems related to domains of language, motor development, and social skills (Center for Early Education and Development, 1990; Howe & Howze, 1989; Lumsden, 1990; Pinkerton, 1991). The drug-exposed child's ability to cope and to do well in an academic setting is often compromised or diminished, as a result of these impairments. The classroom teacher's attitude toward the child, however, may be a decisive or significant influence on how well the child ultimately performs and how the child succeeds in overcoming his or her deficiencies.

ATTITUDES AND TEACHER ATTITUDES

Attitude has been defined as "the intensity of positive or negative affect for or against a psychological object" (Thurstone, 1946, p.39). It has similarly been defined as "a psychological tendency that is expressed by evaluating a particular entity with some degree of favor or disfavor" (Eagly & Chaiken, 1993, p.1); or as Emory Bogardus states, "an attitude is a tendency to act toward or against some environmental factor" (1931, p.45). Although definitions of attitude vary, it is generally defined in operational terms as a "response to some object along a bipolar evaluative dimension" (Eiser, 1987, p.3).

As a psychological construct attitude cannot be measured directly but it can denote an inferred position on an affective continuum (Henerson, Morris, & Fitz-Gibbon, 1978; Mueller, 1986). Once an attitudinal object is identified, an individual will tend to respond with some favorable or unfavorable behavior or position toward that object. The indicated position originates internally, while the evaluative response may be "overt or covert, cognitive, affective, or behavioral"

(Eagly & Chaiken, 1993, p.1). The affective component of the response reflects the person's emotions, the liking, or feelings toward an object. The cognitive component of an attitudinal response comprises the person's thoughts, beliefs, or actual knowledge about the object. The behavioral dimension of an attitude involves the action directed toward the psychological object (Eagly & Chaiken, 1993; Zimbardo, Ebbesen & Maslach, 1977).

Teachers' attitudes toward their students will reflect itself along a continuum of favorability (Henerson, Morris & Fitz-Gibbon, 1978). These attitudes dictate the teachers' behavior based upon the beliefs that the individual teacher holds.

Teacher expectations also evolve from teachers' beliefs. When teachers are susceptible to specific beliefs about a child they typically will behave in a manner that reflects those beliefs (Nieto, 1992, Rosenthal & Jacobs, 1968).

In the student-teacher relationship, how do the variables such as teacher training and years of experience affect the development of favorable or unfavorable attitudes toward cocaine-exposed children? What role does the specialization of Special Education play in the development of teachers' attitudes toward drug-related births? A special education teacher's preparation brings greater exposure to a wider range of individual differences among children. The length of time in the special education forum may also play a role in the formation of the attitudes of these teachers. These are the underlying issues that are under investigation in this study.

DISABILITIES AND THE LAW

Legal directives have already been established for inclusion of children with disabilities with typically developing children in school programs (Public Law 99-457 which has been reauthorized as PL 102-119 the Individuals with Disabilities Education Act-IDEA), and adequate support services must accompany these directives if the target population of children with special needs is to be properly served. Presumably children born to maternal cocaine users are entitled to special education services if they show signs of developmental delays or disabilities. Given the current federal legislation, more knowledge about teachers' attitudes toward drug-exposed children who may exhibit atypical development is warranted.

Attitudes of teachers toward special education populations, which is the focus of this study, have been examined in other research studies, and the findings have generally supported the conclusion that, when compared with special education teachers, non-special education teachers tend to exhibit a more negative attitude toward children with special education needs (Anderson, 1993; Criswell, 1993). Teachers with less information and training in special-needs education and less interactive experience with special-needs children, will usually exhibit less favorable attitudes. Jenkins (1991) discusses the importance of positive attitudes toward children with special needs and the shifts that may occur when negative expectations are minimized with additional support and training. This body of research literature led me to believe that similar differences may be apparent toward drug-exposed children.

PURPOSE AND HYPOTHESES

The proposed study is a descriptive study using survey methodology initiated to measure and compare the attitudes of two naturally occurring groups of teachers. The central elements are: 1) the attitudinal construct, that is, children of drug-related births; and 2) an attempt to determine the attitude of teachers whose specific training and experience varies concerning children with special needs. In an attempt to respond to these questions, the following hypothesis will be tested:

Teachers with training and experience in special education will hold more favorable attitudes toward children of crack/cocaine-related births in comparison to teachers without specific special-education training and experience.

This hypothesis is expected to answer the following questions; 1) Does teacher training and/or years of experience have an affect on teacher attitudes toward and expectations about special-education students? 2) If so, to what extent does teacher training influence attitudes toward drug-related births with special needs?

CONCEPTUAL FRAMEWORK

This study examines the attitudes of educators toward children of drug-related births and the effect of prior preparation or training and experience in special education on those attitudes within the educational environment.

The conceptual framework designed for this study evolved from the theoretical perspectives yielded by the ecological model of child and school functioning (Bronfenbrenner, 1986) and the psychological construct of attitude (Mueller, 1986). It has been informed also by an investigation of teacher expectations (Rosenthal & Jacobs, 1968; Rubovits & Maher, 1973; Dotts, 1978)) and the effect of those expectations on the teachers' behavior and on environments created for the students.

This model has been developed based on a theoretical understanding of the impact of environmental factors (e.g., values and beliefs as well as educational training and experience) on the educators' attitudes toward the child (i.e., positive, negative, or neutral) and, consequently, the impact of teacher attitudes on the child's sense of vulnerability and subsequent behavior (i.e., responsive, nonresponsive) over time (Bronfenbrenner, 1979; Eagly & Chaiken, 1993; Lewis & Bendersky, 1995; Mueller, 1986).

The graphic representation in Figure 1.1 illustrates the relationship among the four tiers of the study. A four-tiered conceptual framework, derived from the perspective of ecological psychology guides the research approach. First, it has been stated that behavior evolves as a function of the interplay between person and environment, and that in order to understand the behavior of individuals, their environments have to be examined (Bronfenbrenner, 1979). In the case of the children of drug-related births, this bi-directional affiliation begins prenatally with the fetus's relationship to its mother and to the chemical. The behavior-shaping affiliation between child and environment continues within the microsystem of the child with medical personnel, family, school and community relationships, which are all involved in a series of transactions or interactions (Bronfenbrenner, 1979; Lewin, 1935). Second, it has been documented that attitudes are based on values and beliefs, within the mesosystem, and that teachers' attitudes and interactions toward students vary based upon individual expectations and prior experiences (Bronfenbrenner, 1979; Eagly & Chaiken, 1993). Third, children born into stressful situations or lifestyles may encounter even more destablilizers in a nonsupportive macrosystem and exosystem (Lewis & Bendersky, 1995; Poulsen, 1991). Fourth, connections with the media, relationships with the extended family and friends, socio-economic resources, and specifically for the student, the classroom teacher's training and exposure can generate conflict or resiliency (Werner, 1994). This patterning of life events and transitions occurs within the child as well as within the environment (Bronfenbrenner, 1986). These are events that are out of the control of

the developing child and that affect the individual over an extended
period of time.

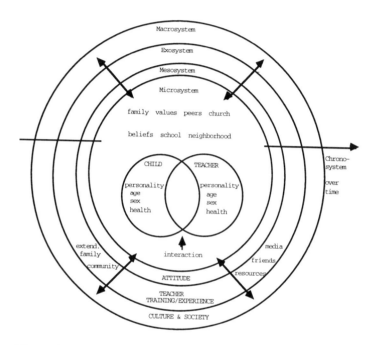

Figure 1.1 Conceptual Framework for Study

SIGNIFICANCE OF STUDY

To the author's knowledge, the present study is the first study
conducted of teachers' attitudes toward drug-related births. The tested
hypothesis yields information on whether teachers with specific
training and experience in working with children with special needs are
more favorable in their attitudes toward drug-related births. It also
yields data on the implications of those attitudes for intervention, staff
development, and educational policy. The study expands our
understanding of some critical issues of the educational process for
children with special needs. This includes the attitude of the teacher, the
influence of attitude on the interaction between the teacher and student,

and the role of specialized education in the education process for special-needs children.

It is hoped that this study will serve as a catalyst for school districts to develop plans for educating teachers and administrators about the special needs of drug-exposed children. It will also be instrumental for curriculum and policy planning and development in preservice educational institutions. The results of this study will assist in developing such training, as the findings yield information on teachers' attitudes toward drug-exposed children. The training can then address such attitudes while alerting educators to the
actual (versus expected) needs of drug-exposed children in the regular classroom (Lumsden, 1990).

Instrument development of the ATDB was an important outcome of the study. The development and testing of a reliable instrument for future testing this population will be beneficial to other research studies.

CHAPTER II

Review of the Literature

This review of the literature examines teacher attitudes and the effects of prenatal drug exposure. Every individual exhibits an attitude toward some object, and that attitude will conceivably manifest itself on a continuum as either favorable, neutral, or nonfavorable (Henerson, Morris, & Fitz-Gibbon, 1978). An instructor's attitude "is the tendency to act toward or against some environmental factor" (Bogardus, 1931, p.45). In the classroom, the instructor's attitudes tend to result in specific behaviors toward students, and that behavior will stem from the beliefs that comprise the teacher's attitudes. If instructors hold favorable beliefs about their students and consider them "likable," then their response to belief statements about the children will demonstrate a positive attitude (Eagly & Chaiken, 1993).

Historically, studies of teacher expectations indicate that students and teachers perform in response to projected expectations (Rosenthal & Jacobs, 1968). In situations where teachers had inaccurate information concerning their students' abilities, the teachers modified their expectations and instructional behaviors accordingly. The teachers displayed distinctly favorably-biased behavior toward those students who the false reports designated as more capable.

More recent research has focused on how teacher expectations vary with students' social class or race (Nieto, 1992). While this research is not without controversy, it continues to provide supporting evidence for the position of the influence of teachers' preconceived perceptions, on both teacher and subsequent student performance. In instances where teachers were presented with a profile of the "ideal" student at the beginning of the schoolyear, it was found that they maintained specific expectations of students who would fit the profile and the ones who did not. Throughout the year, the manifestation of differential treatment for the two student profiles was observed (Nieto, 1992).

Experiments involving racial differences have produced similar conclusions. Rubovitz & Maher (1973) report that teachers' expectations were mediated by individual stereotypes, and when unknowingly presented with students of comparable ability, they gave preferential treatment to white students designated as "gifted" over black students similarly designated.

An investigation by Dotts (1978) on teacher attitudes towards poverty and the disadvantaged provides further evidence of differentiation of treatment of students on the basis of attitudes. The study of fifty-one black (n=24) and white (n=27) teachers examined attitudes in elementary schools as a vehicle to improve pre-service and inservice training. The investigation used a questionnaire to examine the possible impact of low teacher expectations. The results support the conclusion that teachers often do discriminate against disadvantaged students and simultaneously hold pessimistic expectations of this student population.

A meta-analysis of the basis of teacher expectations (Dusek, & Joseph, 1983) further illustrates the propensity toward discriminatory behavior toward students. A similar bias was found when seventy-seven studies were reviewed for discrepancies in teacher expectations. The analysis investigated teacher expectations of students based upon three attributes: physical attributes, social class, and behavior labels. In terms of physical attributes it was found that in seven of the eleven studies, teachers expected physically attractive students to perform better academically. This determinant of attractiveness was a prevalent expectation for academic performance and social/personality attributes.

A study (Dusek & Joseph, 1983) of twenty-four elementary classrooms revealed specific patterns of differences in reinforcement which favored middle-class students over lower-class students. Most of this disparate reinforcement was nonverbal attention in the form of offering assistance or more attention to middle-class students. A third aspect of the analysis examined expectancies for students with behavior labels or descriptors (e.g., LD-Learning Disabled). It was found that such "deviancy labels resulted in negative expectancies" when teachers were asked to predict the child's skill level and academic future (Dusek & Joseph, 1983, p.333). This lends support to the adverse effects of low teacher expectations when there is a use of labels.

Issues surrounding the behavior of teachers with negative attitudes toward special-needs students indicate a likelihood to engage in unequal treatment of these students. Studies (Knoff, 1985; Stephens & Braun, 1980) demonstrate that teachers often display negative attitudes when asked to work with special-needs students in their classrooms.

Knoff (1985) surveyed 200 special and 200 non-special educators by administering a 30 item questionnaire regarding placement of special education students. Seventy-nine percent of the participants gave a negative response to the item asking if special education was phased out, would non-special education teachers be willing to accept the special needs students into their classrooms.

Stephens and Braun (1980) administered a 20 item scale to measure the willingness of 795 non-special education teachers to reintegrate handicapped children into their classes. Almost forty percent of the teachers indicated they were unwilling to reintegrate the special-needs students into their classrooms.

A study by Nord, Good, & Shinn (1992) on teacher attitudes toward the reintegration of learning-disabled children was consistent with prior research that indicates the unenthusiastic or neutral attitude of regular classroom teachers to reintegration. Twenty-six teachers were divided into two groups based on their students, some of whom held the potential for reintegration and others who did not. The teachers were not given any other specific student information (e.g. achievement test scores) and were given a test (i.e., Teacher Attitudes Toward Reintegration Pre/Post Data Questionnaire) to assess their general attitude toward the reintegration of learning-disabled students into their classrooms. Four weeks later, they were given student test scores and other evaluation information (e.g., Woodcock-Johnson, curriculum-based measures) and then tested on their attitudes. It was found that upon receiving the additional information, their attitude responses shifted and became more favorable toward integration of the special needs students into their classrooms.

In a small study of teachers (n=5), Jenkins (1991) found low interaction rates between regular classroom teachers and special-needs students when contrasted with the rates between special-education teachers and the same students. Although this study was limited by the sample size, it was able to demonstrate a relationship between teacher attitude and teacher behavior toward special-needs students. The results supported the hypothesis that special education teachers would interact more with the special needs students than would the non-special education teachers.

Studies on teacher attitudes do not always indicate uniformly negative attitudes toward special-education students or integrated classrooms. Attitudes are in practice often more complex or ambiguous than they may seem. Non-special education teachers were more rejecting of special education students who were learning disabled, yet, many of these teachers in existing inclusion situations expressed a concern for these children while simultaneously evincing an attitude of rejection (Siegel & Moore, 1994).

A 25 item questionnaire was administered to 334 certified school personnel in Mississippi, on the overall attitude toward special education. Attitudes were moderately positive within that group, however, regular classroom teachers and vocational-education teachers were found to have the least favorable attitudes toward special education students (Anderson, Criswell, Slate & Jones, 1993).

Many regular classroom teachers report that they believe their training to be inadequate for working with special-needs children (Anderson, Criswell, Slate & Jones, 1993; Fulk & Hirt, 1994; Jenkins, 1991). Many indicate that special-education teachers would better serve this population in separate classrooms (Siegel & Norbert, 1994). Many systems do not require teachers to take special-education training/coursework en route to certification, and these teachers may feel underprepared to address the task of working with the atypical student. Fulk & Hirth (1994) conducted a study in which 517 teachers were asked to provide a self-evaluation of their skill levels for working with regular and special-education students. They found that teachers reported significant differences in competency in teaching the two populations, with the highest level of inadequacy reported for working with students with disabilities.

Criswell, Anderson, Slate, & Jones (1993), survey 174 school personnel and found special education teachers had a more favorable attitude toward special-needs students. While non-special education teachers of grades 3-6 held more positive attitudes than the others.

Although it appears that teachers' attitudes can affect their behavior toward a student, little is known about teachers' attitudes toward children born to substance abusers. These children often enter school surrounded by a barrage of negative media exposure and preceded by labeling by society at large. For example, the eye-catching headlines and images of drug use constructed by the media have not been supported by the research, yet they play an integral role in the perceptions formed by members of the community and the macroculture (Poulsen, 1992; Zuckerman, Frank & Brown, 1995). Judith Burnison (1991) states that many teachers and administrators are anxious, perhaps even fearful, about having such children in their schools. Recent media stories have depicted drug-exposed children as uneducable, a "lost generation"; "born to lose"; "no hope babies" and "the bio-underclass" (Zuckerman, Frank & Brown, 1995). This damage must be evaluated and if necessary, reversed and terminated (Burnison, 1991; Poulsen, 1991). A growing fear is that this portrayal of children born to substance abusers will create a self-fulfilling prophecy, particularly if the encouraging findings are minimized or dismissed.

Erroneous or sensationalized information concerning children of drug-related births is prone to generating negative teacher attitudes that lead to suboptimal behavior toward the students. Since the preliminary findings about the development of these children indicate a wide range of possible developmental outcomes, they should not be inadvertently or prematurely classified as incompetent (Howard, 1991; Howard & O'Donnell,1995). In contrast to the paucity of information about teacher attitudes toward drug-exposed children, there is some research data, though limited, on the developmental progress of such children. The degree of trauma experienced by drug-exposed children prenatally varies in intensity and frequency, and the resulting developmental impact is equally varied. Many of these children will appear to develop typically and their drug history may appear insignificant; however, there are many children who have pronounced impairments and it is critical that their special needs be understood and addressed, without the additional burden of a teacher's negative attitude.

PRENATAL DRUG USE AND SPECIAL POPULATIONS

The literature on the increase of substance abuse among adults and the effect of drugs on the adult's physiology is well documented. Research on prenatal exposure, specifically crack/cocaine, is expanding; there are increasing numbers of studies on early intervention, reviews of infant hospital records, and longitudinal studies. The studies examined for this project (see Table 2.1) varied in the number of subjects and the nature of their drug exposure, as well as in the specific outcomes observed. This body of literature also explores the perception that drug-exposed

Table 2.1: Descriptive Summary of Literature Findings

Study	Sample	Perinatal Status	Neurological Status	Cognitive Behavior	Soc-Emotional Behavior	Motor Behavior
Colmorgen 1988	age= Newborn char= PDE n=1088 char= NE n=150	Low birthweight	premature birth			
Chasnoff 1989	age= Newborn char= CE n=70 char= NE n=70	Low birthweight, smaller head circumference, growth morbidity, growth retardation, premature birth	Gaze aversion Microcephaly		Inability to moderate arousal. Easily overstimulated.	NBAS=poor motor, poor orientation, Poor muscle tone
Chasnoff, et al 1989	age=Newborn char= CE n=75 char= NE n=40	Low birthweight, shorter length, smaller head circumference	Small cranium		Inability to moderate arousal	NBAS=poor motor, poor orientation

Note. CE= Cocaine Exposed   DE= Drug Exposed   PDE= Polydrug Exposed   NE= Not Exposed   A= Addicted   NA= Not Addicted

Table 2.1 (continued)

Study	Sample	Perinatal Status	Neurological Status	Cognitive Behavior	Soc-Emotional Behavior	Motor Behavior
Kaye, Elkind, Goldberg, Tytun 1989	age= Newborn char= PDE n=585 char= NE n=560	Low birthweight	premature birth withdrawal			
Van Baar 1989	age= 30 mos char= DE n=35 char= NE n=37			delayed language	tense	poor coordination
Zuckerman, et al 1989	age= Newborn char= CE n=114 char= NE n=202	Low birthweight, shorter length	Small cranium			
Deoliveira, Bryant 1991	age= 2mos + char= CE n=10		premature birth	communication delays Inability to moderate arousal	feeding problems	motor delays hypertonicity
Lester, et al 1991	age= Newborn char= CE n=80 char= NE n=80	Low birthweight, shorter length.	Prenatal synaptic alterations		Patterns of excitable and depressed. High pitched cry.	Hypertonicity

Note. CE= Cocaine Exposed DE= Drug Exposed PDE= Polydrug Exposed NE= Not Exposed A= Addicted NA= Not Addicted

Table 2.1 (continued)

Study	Sample	Perinatal Status	Neurological Status	Cognitive Behavior	Soc-Emotional Behavior	Motor Behavior
Select Committee on Narcotics Abuse and Control 1991	age= Newborn char= CE n=1900		Premature birth Autism	Delays in language Short attention span	Explosive behavior, poor transitions, indiscriminate attachments, feeding disorders	
Chasnoff, et al 1992	age=2 char= PDE n=106 char= PDE n=45 char= NE n=81	smaller head circumference, shorter length		MDI=lower mean scores		PDI=lower mean scores
Chasnoff, Griffith, Freier, Murray 1992	age=2 char= DE n=106 char= PDE ≠cocaine n=45 char= NE n=81		small cranium		poor regulation	

Note. CE= Cocaine Exposed   DE= Drug Exposed   PDE= Polydrug Exposed   NE= Not Exposed   A= Addicted   NA= Not Addicted

Table 2.1 (continued)

Study	Sample	Perinatal Status	Neurological Status	Cognitive Behavior	Soc-Emotional Behavior	Motor Behavior
Lawley 1992	age= 3.2 char= A n=25 char= NA n=25			Overall lower development	Increased crying in infant poor eating	
National Health Consortium 1992	age= Newborn + 18 char= DE n=18	Easily overstimulated, aggressive or laconic		Language problems poor attention and poor organizational skills	Less securely attached, impulsive, constricted play.	
Bateman, Ng, Hansen, Heagarty 1993	age= Newborn char= CE n=361 char=NE n=387	Low birthweight decreased length	Small cranium			
Woods, Eyler, Behnke, Conlon 1993	age= Newborn char= CE n=35 char=NE n=35	Low birthweight shorter gestation				
Griffith, Azuma, Chasnoff 1994	age= 3 char= CE n=93 char= PDE n=24 char= NE n=25	smaller head circumference		low verbal reasoning	aggressive externalizing behavior	

Note. CE= Cocaine Exposed   DE= Drug Exposed   PDE= Polydrug Exposed   NE= Not Exposed   A= Addicted   NA= Not Addicted

children have created a special population. The studies discussed here are organized on the basis of the chronological age of the target children.

DEFINITIONS OF DRUG-RELATED BIRTHS AND THE EFFECTS

What is a drug-related birth? The definition of drug-related births in the literature varies considerably with the type of the drug exposure. Attempts to come up with a definition for infants exposed to just one drug, such as alcohol, may result in a specific definition such as "alcohol-exposed infants." This may generate an effect label such as Fetal Alcohol Syndrome. However, infants exposed to chemicals in utero are often the victims of more than one drug and are therefore defined as polydrug-exposed. Hence the ambiguity surrounding what is often too general a definition.

The effects of drugs on the developing fetus also vary greatly. In some cases, the newborn is born addicted and goes through withdrawal but does not otherwise demonstrate any difficulties later in life. Indeed, Zuckerman (1991) cautions that special care must be taken not to automatically assume that an infant who goes through withdrawal will therefore experience neurobehavioral dysfunction. In other cases, the toxicity of exposure may lead to direct injury to the infant. Such injury on the one hand, may have immediate developmental consequences; on the other hand it may not cause visible effects until the child enters specific developmental periods. Factors that account for the variability in the effects of exposure include the complex way in which drugs affect an infant's physiology; the time or frequency; and the dosage and drug quality of each exposure (Weston, Ivins, Zuckerman, Jones & Lopez, 1989).

Effects of drug use on the fetus may be either direct or indirect. Researchers define direct effects as those that occur as a result of one or more drugs passing through the placenta. Direct effects result in an accumulation of neurotransmitters around the receptors of the fetal brain during synaptic transmission. The outcome of this disruption of neurochemicals, is an increase in blood pressure, a predisposition to irregular heartbeat, and seizures. By contrast, indirect effects are those that can be attributed to changes in the environment of the fetus and in the mother's central nervous system that create a risk for the fetus (Lester et. al, 1991; Lewis & Bendersky, 1995; Weiss, Mirin & Bartel,

1994; Weston, Ivins, Zuckerman, Jones & Lopez, 1989; Zuckerman, 1991). One of the primary effects attributable to such changes is a decrease in the flow of oxygen and nutrients to the fetus. Although the blood vessels in the fetal environment are usually dilated during pregnancy, the introduction of cocaine into the system causes these vessels to constrict (Jacques & Snyder, 1991; Leavitt, 1995). The resultant interruption of oxygen and nutrient flow may affect tissue development in the fetus during early gestation and cause the deformation of developing organs such as the kidneys. It has been speculated that vasoconstriction, increased blood pressure, and other direct and indirect effects of drug ingestion may induce preterm labor, precipitous labor, and abruptio placenta as well as explain growth retardation in some drug-exposed infants (Chasnoff, 1992; Lewis & Bendersky, 1995; Weiss, Mirin & Bartel, 1994).

Perinatal insult may occur through the infant's ingestion of breast milk from a cocaine abusing mother. Cocaine has been found to remain in breast milk for up to four days or longer after drug use. These drug-exposed infants may present hypertension, tachycardia, sweating and pupil dilation (Gold, 1993).

None of the explanations exclude the possibility of damage to the infant and thus the term "drug-related" and "drug-exposed" will be used in this study to mean that the infant was born with some level of chemicals in his or her system at birth. The magnitude of that exposure is accepted as variable and inconsistent.

PRENATAL AND PERINATAL EFFECTS OF COCAINE EXPOSURE

Cocaine is easily diffused across the placenta, "achieving peak levels in three minutes" (Gingras, Weese-Mayer, Hume, & O'Donnell, 1992, p.5). Despite this rapid diffusion, the rate of metabolism is much slower in the fetus than it is in the mother and may remain in the infant's system for up to four days. Within twenty-five days after conception, the basic structure of the central nervous system is recognizable and is differentiated from other organ systems. During organogenesis (the first 60 days), the embryo is especially vulnerable to chemical injury that causes structural malformations (Gingras, Weese-Mayer, Hume, & O'Donnell, 1992; Snodgrass, 1994). This damage can express itself in the form of structural malformations of the eyes, kidneys, liver and other critical organs (Poulsen, 1991). Because the developing organ cells migrate and differentiate at a different pace, and because their vulnerability to insult depends upon the developmental phase of the organ, the type of malformation that occurs depends on the phase of organ development at the time of exposure.

Cocaine, for example, appears to cause alterations in regions of the brain which are undergoing synapse formation at the time of drug exposure, thus interfering with developmental processes (Chasnoff, 1992; Lester, et. al., 1991; Mayes, 1994). Such infraction, when it takes place during cell proliferation, cell migration, and organization of brain development is what potentially creates various structural, biological vulnerabilities for the fetus (Lewis & Bendersky, 1995).

There are many risks for a developing fetus with large concentrations of cocaine in the brain. The period from the eighth week after conception to birth is a time of increased neurological development and general fetal activity. This is the time when intrauterine growth retardation and other physiological and behavioral deficits may result if there is exposure to teratogens such as cocaine (Cole & Cole, 1993). Cocaine is also known to affect the developing endocrine system of the infant. The endocrine system significantly influences brain development, and the stimulation of abnormal hormonal secretions can adversely affect brain structure and function by disrupting the growth processes of brain neurons. Any incidence of toxic exposure during development can hinder the healthy developmental process of neurons. Brain function entails the interaction of several mechanisms which develop at different rates and times during gestation. The introduction of toxic substances can alter the cell structure, often resulting in swelling, an increase in acidity, or inhibited neurotransmitter secretions within the cells. Neurons require large quantities of oxygen and are vulnerable to oxygen deprivation or "anoxia" (OTA, 1990). Neurotransmitters play a critical role in basic processes such as state regulation, and interference in their circulation may lead to poor responsiveness in the infant (Chasnoff, 1992; Lewis & Bendersky, 1995). Abnormal neural growth, differentiation, ectopic cells during migration, and abnormal glial cell functions are possible during these vulnerable periods.

An acute toxic effect of cocaine in the central nervous system typically results in microcephaly or a small cranium, prematurity, low gestational weight and other neurobehavioral dysfunctions (Barton, Harrigan & Tse, 1995; Chasnoff, 1989; Snodgrass, 1994; Woods et al, 1993; Zuckerman, 1989;). The increased incidence of small cranium and abnormal neurofunctions such as "prolonged auditory evoked response" suggests delayed myelination and altered DNA and supports the concept of injury to the developing fetal brain by cocaine. The excitable cry of cocaine-exposed infants may be related to the direct effects of the substance on their brain, and the depressed cry is believed to be a result of indirect effects (Lewis & Bendersky, 1995).

The hippocampus, a major component of the limbic system, works with the hypothalamus and amygdala to control mood, emotion, and motivation. The hippocampus is important to learning and memory, and these processes can sustain serious impairment if the hippocampus or relevant nerve pathways are destroyed or damaged. It is believed that the hippocampus is a primary target of many toxic substances, which may disrupt the delicate balance between these cells and the neurotransmitters. When excitatory neurotransmitters are released by neurons and flood neighboring cells, the cell membranes are weakened and cell death occurs (Chasnoff, 1992; OTA, 1990).

NEUROLOGICAL STRUCTURE AND EFFECTS OF PRENATAL COCAINE EXPOSURE

The effect of cocaine use by pregnant women on their infants has recently become a target of investigation. Most of the early research focused on pregnancy complications and early infant trauma. High incidence of spontaneous abortion, abruptio placenta, and premature delivery were markers of this research (Chasnoff, 1976). More recently researchers (Barton, Harrigan & Tse, 1995; Chasnoff, 1989; Chasnoff, et al, 1989; Chasnoff, 1992) have confirmed these findings and have also found that drug-exposed infants have a lower mean gestational age, smaller craniums, impaired motor orientation, and deficient state regulation behavior when compared to control infants. Cocaine-exposed infants are easily overstimulated by light and noise and have a poor response to cuddling and stroking. These infants may demonstrate increased tone or arching (hypertonicity) when attempts are made to nestle them closely (Poulsen, 1991).

Another study reported by Chavez, Mulinare, & Cordero (1989), suggests that congenital urogenital anomalies result from cocaine use by pregnant abusers. The study, conducted in Atlanta, found a total of 1,067 cases of urinary and genital anomalies over a twelve-year period. Maternal cocaine use was defined as ingestion anywhere from one month prior to pregnancy through the first trimester. These results were supported also by Zuckerman et al. (1991).

An early study (Chasnoff, 1976) consisted of 75 pregnant women who had similar drug-use patterns and demographics. The newborns were evaluated using traditional scales such as the Neonatal Behavioral Assessment Scale (NBAS) and the Ballard evaluation. The infants of the mothers who used cocaine only through the first trimester demonstrated fewer developmental deficiencies than those infants whose mothers continued to abuse the drug throughout the pregnancy. Overall, exposed infants demonstrated evidence of seizures, cerebral infarctions, and genitourinary tract abnormalities.

Chasnoff (1989) continued to study these infants and reported that at one month the infants had made significant improvements in their ability to regulate their arousal. Yet they were still responding at levels below that of drug-free babies. Many of these infants required special assistance by the caretaker in order to remain stable during stimulation. Difficulties with muscle tone persisted in some infants through the fourth month.

The results of a two year follow-up study of 106 infants of polydrug users, and 81 nonexposed infants indicated similar developmental difficulties to those reported by Chasnoff and colleagues (1989) on newborns. The results indicated significantly smaller head circumference, developmental delays, and shorter body length for the drug-exposed infants, thus suggesting persistent developmental damage (Bateman, Ng, Hansen & Heagarty, 1993; Gonzalez & Campbell, 1994; Lester et al, 1991; Van Baar, 1989; Zuckerman et al, 1989).

These results were supported by Zuckerman et. al (1989), who used urine assays of 114 cocaine abusers to acquire a drug-exposed sample. Interviews were conducted with the participants and consent was received to analyze the urine samples for drugs. The study found that those women who abused cocaine delivered infants with low birthweight, shorter body length, and smaller head circumference. The reliability of the study was enchanced by the use of assays since some of the mothers denied drug use in their self report yet tested positive with the urine analysis. The infants of these mothers who tested positive but denied drug-use displayed characteristics of the drug-exposed infants. Similarly, a larger study (n=1,226) of low-income, minority mothers found that 114 babies tested positive in urine assays, and that they had significantly lower birthweight, smaller head circumference, and shorter body length (Cook, Petersen & Moore, 1990; Hurt, et al., 1996; Sallee et al., 1995).

In 1989, in another evaluation of polydrug use, researchers analyzed the records of 585 infants registered in the Infant Health Assessment Program in New York to determine drug exposure and the effects of exposure. The birth records of crack/cocaine and polydrug-exposed infants were compared to those of drug-free infants. The neurological outcomes for crack-exposed infants appeared to be the most severe (Kaye, Elkind, Goldberg, & Tytun, 1989). The similarities between this study and others (Chapman, Elliott, 1995; Colmorgen, 1988; Lester et al, 1991) highlight some of the developmental outcomes confounded by polydrug use.

The research continues to unveil new knowledge on substance abuse and its effect on child development. Prevalent neurological findings include tremors, excessive high-pitched crying, hyperactivity, and irritability (Lester et al., 1991; Lewis & Bendersky, 1995). Exposed infants are generally "lethargic and poorly responsive, hypertonic when alert, tremulous, and disorganized in sleeping and feeding" (Dixon, Bresnahan, & Zuckerman, 1990, p. 81).

Low birthweight is another consistent finding in research on drug-exposed infants (Bateman, Ng, Hansen & Heagarty, 1993; Chasnoff, 1989; Colmorgen, 1988; Kaye, Elkind, Goldberg & Tytun, 1989; Lester et al, 1991). One cause with which low-birthweight has been associated is the "appetite suppressing characteristics" of cocaine and its subsequent contribution to poor maternal nutrition (Cook, Petersen & Moore, 1990). The interaction of illicit drugs with illness poses another conceivable compromise for the health of the infant (Lewis & Bendersky, 1995).

The literature suggests that proper brain growth and development bear a direct relationship with developmental issues that the infants will later encounter (Griffith, Azuma, Chasnoff, 1992; Kronstadt, 1991). Recent studies indicate that infants of drug-related births are born not only with smaller craniums but also with less dense brain tissue (Davis, 1992; Cook, Peterson & Moore, 1990; Jacques & Snyder, 1991; Zuckerman, 1991). This is of concern because children who are severely microcephalic have been shown to have poor processing skills (Davis et al, 1992; Kronstadt, 1991; Zuckerman, 1991). Infants with smaller craniums therefore have a high probability of smaller brain development. A small cranium is a consistent finding in the research, as is premature birth (Chasnoff, 1989; Chasnoff et al, 1989; Colmorgen,

1988; Kaye, Elkind, Goldberg & Tytun, 1989; Bateman, Ng & Heagarty, 1993).

A study of the ability of drug-exposed infants to learn was conducted by Alessandri, Sullivan, Imaizumi, & Lewis (1993). Of the infants in this study (n=72) who were aged 4-8 months, half had been exposed to cocaine and half served as controls. The exposed infants had lower birth weight and were shorter in body length than the nonexposed group. The infants were observed in an arm-pulling activity, and evaluated initially to determine a baseline. They were then evaluated in their learning phase of the arm pulling activity, which provided a visual and musical response to their pulls on an attached string. Third, the study evaluated the infants' reaction to the extinction or cessation of payoffs (the visuals and singing) for making the gestures was the third evaluative piece. Finally, the researchers looked to see if the infants would make a second learning attempt. All activities and attempts were recorded on video. The major differences between the groups were 1) the cocaine-exposed infants were not as aroused and had a lower mean arm-pull rate; 2) they also expressed fewer positive emotion such as joy; 3) there was little response when the extinction point of the activity was reached, thus no second attempt at learning was made. This depressed performance was consistent at 4, 6, and 8 months, which suggests a persistence of deficiencies in arousal and emotional responsivity over time.

These initial difficulties in the infant's life can present the first problems for parenting, particularly with those infants who demonstrate diminished interactive capabilities and gaze aversion. Due to poor oculomotor coordination, a simple task of following a slow moving object, may prove to be too difficult for the infant (Jones, 1991; Poulsen, 1991).

ENVIRONMENTAL EFFECTS

Some researchers (Colmorgen, 1988; Lester et al, 1991) attempted to distinguish their outcomes with consideration to lifestyle and environmental factors of the abusers. Their research specifically highlighted the manner in which drug-users will indulge in whatever substance to which they have access, including alcohol cigarettes, and other illicit drugs. The postnatal environment is also an issue in determining the opportunity for adequate development of the fetus. This environment is defined as the psychological and social factors of substance abusing lifestyle and the distressed atmosphere to which these drug-exposed children are subjected. The importance of this social environment is its often dubious influence on these childrens' lives. "The single most important influence on developmental outcome of the child with high needs and low threshold is the psychosocial environment in which the child is reared" (Poulsen, 1991, p.13). Many drug-exposed infants must also contend with parental neglect and other parental stresses (Weston, Ivins, Zuckerman, Jones & Lopez, 1989), while grappling with poor nutrition, exposure to infectious disease, poverty, exposure to crime and violence, and a chaotic lifestyle or homelessness (Lewis & Bendersky, 1995; Poulsen, 1991; Vincent, 1991; Zuckerman, Frank & Brown, 1995).

The dyadic relationship of the drug abusing mother and her infant may be impaired in a variety of ways. A recent study by Burns, Chethik, Burns, & Clark (1991) of five abusing mothers, whose interactions with their infants were videotaped, illustrated several significant areas of concern. These areas included: the mother's and infant's lack of initiative and resourcefulness; the infant's lack of cheerfulness; and the lack of mutual enjoyment in the dyad. Additional concerns were the mother's failure to provide structure and routine and an insensitivity and overintrusiveness. As these infants mature, the difficulties of parenting may escalate with the additional developmental difficulties.

BEHAVIORAL EFFECTS OF PRENATAL COCAINE EXPOSURE

The early and long term effects of cocaine on the developing child are diverse. While many of these children appear typical at birth, it has been observed that there are some developmental deficits that may require drug-exposed children to require nontraditional approaches to their integration into social interactions. "As they mature, some affected children seem to "outgrow" the developmental difficulties seen at birth, such as tremors, but they continue to show impaired abilities to concentrate, relate to peers in group settings, and cope with unstructured environment" (National Association of State Directors of Special Education, 1992, p.2).

Research conducted on drug-exposed toddlers (12-30 mos) indicate less age-appropriate play, high rates of indiscriminate and disorganized attachment, insecure attachment, language and behavioral problems, and easy frustration and distractibility (Jones, 1991; Kronstadt, 1991; Rodning, Beckwith & Howard, 1989; 1992). The Rodning study showed a lower representation of play events by the drug-exposed group of children (n=18) than the nonexposed group (n=23). At three years of age language problems and organizational skills were still poorly established (Kronstadt, 1991; van Baar, 1989; Waller, 1992).

Other literature (National Health/Education Consortium, 1991) indicates that prenatal cocaine exposure in infants has an influence on learning and memory. Kronstadt (1991) predicts an intense need for attention by these children in the classroom to compensate for these deficits. Burnison (1991) states that in the sixth year of the NAPARE longitudinal study of 300 prenatally drug-exposed infants, it was found that almost all of these children can process information and learn despite neurobehavioral deficiencies, language and attention difficulties, and self-regulatory problems.

Developmental delays in a retrospective chart study of 70 children, ranging in age from birth to 30 months, were observed in areas of language, motor skills, social skills and play (Davis, et al 1992). Davis has noted that significant neurodevelopmental abnormalities and a frequency of autism were seen in many of the drug-exposed children. Other studies have indicated that many children of heavy drug-users, while not necessarily mentally retarded, may exhibit signs of learning disabilities (Hawley & Disney, 1992; Howard, 1991). Others have found similar delays and deficiencies in drug-exposed children (Bellisimo, 1990; Van Dyke & Fox, 1990). These behaviors include externalizing behavior problems, attention-deficits and language difficulties. Some of the specific early language skill abnormalities noted were a failure to vocalize other than cry through the fourth month of development, delayed acquisition and limited use of holophrases and telegraphic speech, and long periods of silence. Difficulties with visual motor skills and gross motor delays apparent in spontaneous play have also been noted (Davis, et al, 1992). The range of possible developmental and learning problems suggests that drug-exposed children are predisposed to special education placement.

Shifts in behavioral development may range from labile affect and apathy to aggressiveness and explosive reactions. These children are limited in their attempts to initiate or reciprocate social interactions with eye contact or gestures, while responding to praise or verbal directions (Jones, 1991). This is consequential on the teacher-student bond, since the use of praise and reprimands are often used in educational settings to modulate behavior and facilitate the educational process.

Kronstadt (1991) indicates that most drug-exposed children are from low socioeconomic backgrounds, and prior research has indicated that scores of children from low income groups drop below the norm as the children mature through age three. Lewis & Bendersky (1995) state that drug-exposed children "...are not homogeneous with respect to how they present medically, or with respect to how they present behaviorally (p.33)." They also note how "these different beginnings may result in different developmental trajectories as the exigencies of the caregiving environment come into play (p.33)." However, it must be emphasized that there is no homogeneous group of drug-exposed children. Drug-exposed children are individuals with specific developmental deficiencies and should be treated as such.

Some prenatally drug-exposed children demonstrate a low threshold to incoming sensory and emotional situations, and are easily overwhelmed. Their incapacity to modulate their behavior is often seen as destructive. Drug-exposed children have demonstrated explosive behavior and difficulty adapting to transitions in activities (Lumsden, 1990; Poulsen, 1991; Vincent, 1991). The instances of unpredictable behavior can be bewildering to the unprepared peer/adult. The response of peers and others to their behavior can create a stressful environment for a child who may not possess adequately developed coping mechanisms (Poulsen, 1991). These children also have difficulty with free play, in that they function poorly in comparison to other children in an unstructured situation (Hawley & Disney, 1992; Rist, 1990).

Chasnoff (1989) has documented early indicators of the tendency for these infants to have "hyperexcitable nervous systems" which continue to be apparent in older drug-exposed children. Social interaction problems with peers, and human attachment difficulties are also apparent in school age drug-exposed children (Center for Early Education and Development, 1990; Jones, 1991; Kronstadt, 1991).

It is apparent that teachers' attitudes toward special learning populations has strong impact on the student's education. It has also been documented that parents who use drugs have children who may have special educational needs. Since drug-exposed children have atypical development and behavior which makes them a special population, an important question is; What are teachers' attitudes toward this drug-exposed population?

To answer this question this study was designed to address the following hypothesis:

NULL HYPOTHESIS

Teachers with specific special-education training and experience will hold similar or less favorable attitudes toward children of Crack/cocaine-related births in comparison to teachers without training and experience in special education.

To investigate the hypothesis, a Thurstonian scale was designed in an attempt to investigate the question; Are teachers' attitudes generally unfavorable?; What can we do to eliminate unfavorable attitudes through training?

The Teachers' Attitude Toward Drug Related Births Inventory (ATDB) will be used for attitude assessment (Hubbard, 1994). The instrument is a twenty-item Thurstonian scale, which determines scale values of favorable, neutral, and unfavorable attitudes. The Teachers' Attitude Toward Drug Related Births Inventory will be used in conjunction with the short form of the Marlowe-Crowne Social Desirability Scale (Crowne & Marlowe, 1964). This scale is an instrument which measures the need for approval, which could confound the interpretation of the results of the Teachers' Attitude Toward Drug Related Births Inventory. Administration of the Marlowe-Crowne will indicate whether or not participants respond to scale items as they expect they should instead of truthfully.

CHAPTER III

Methods

This chapter presents the sample and procedure of the method of study. Next, the Attitude Toward Drug-Related Births scale and its development is described, which is followed by a description of the Marlowe-Crowne Social Desirability Scale. The chapter ends with a discussion on the data analyses employed to test the hypothesis.

Sample

School site visits were conducted to solicit participation in the data collection effort. A sample of two self-selected groups were recruited for this study. The sample was comprised of 141 regular classroom teachers and special education teachers, from the New England area schools. These two groups were selected to be diverse in ethnicity and years of experience and were stratified based on teaching experience.

Of the 141 teachers surveyed, 45 were special education teachers, and 96 were regular classroom teachers some of whom were teachers with specializations in areas other than Special Education (e.g. math, science, reading). There was a range of ages in the sample with the median age being 37 years old. The majority of the sample consisted of seasoned teachers with five years or more of teaching experience (see Table 3.1)

As indicated by frequency output and chi-square analysis in Table 3.1, of the total number of teachers, 80 were teachers with an undergraduate degree, and 61 were teachers with a graduate level degree. Over 70% of the teachers had five or more years of teaching experience, and of the total sample, 79% (n=112) were female, while 60% (n=83) were Caucasian.

Some of the subjects reported having had prior drug education coursework (n=40). This includes 29% of the special education teachers (n=17) and 24% of the non-special education teachers (n=23).

SAMPLE SIZE DETERMINATION

The sample size of the study needs to be large enough to detect differences between groups should they exist. The sample size of N=141 was chosen to provide maximum statistical power, and was determined by using four factors: the .05 level of significance; a statistical power of .60; an acceptable effect size of .3 standard deviation; and the analytical procedures of a two group test for independent means (ANOVA or ANCOVA) (Cohen, 1989; Goodwin & Goodwin, 1989; Olejnik, 1984).

The combination of these factors indicates a moderate probability of the sample size of 141 as being significantly large. The .60 level of statistical power implies a sixty percent probability of detecting effects that are at least .3 standard deviations of the population means, while testing a hypothesis with μ =.05 (Cohen, 1989).

Procedure for Sample Recruitment

The study proposal was submitted with an executive summary and the human subjects review board letter of approval, to the Boston Public Schools Office of Planning and Research. Approval from this office then allowed access to the area public schools. A written description of the purpose and design of the research was submitted to school administrators and teachers (see Appendices A and B). The teachers were asked on the consent form to participate on a voluntary basis and were advised that all responses to the instruments were to remain anonymous.

Contact with the principals from several public schools with special education teachers was initiated, and permission was granted to involve the teachers at those schools on a voluntary basis in the study.

Another source of sample population was from three college professors in a local Teacher Education program. All three professors announced that the study was being conducted the following week during the first fifteen minutes of class and that participation was voluntary.

Table 3.1: Total Sample Characteristics

Characteristics	n	%
Gender		
Male	29	20.6
Female	112	79.4
Ethnic Group		
Caucasian	83	58.9
Non-Caucasian	58	41.1
Level of Education		
Undergraduate	80	56.7
Graduate	61	43.3
Years Teaching		
1-4	41	29.1
5-10	43	30.5
11+	57	40.4
Specialty		
Special Education	45	31.9
Non-Special Education	96	68.1

PROCEDURE

Questionnaires were distributed to teachers in envelopes that were put into their public school mailboxes, or distributed at the beginning of their class. The questionnaires required approximately fifteen minutes to complete including the demographics page. The instruction letter indicated that all questionnaires would be collected from a central location in the school, or after the completion of the day's graduate class. (see Appendices A-C)

DEMOGRAPHICS

Information was gathered from the teachers about their age, gender and level of education. The form also asked them to indicate their area of specialization and the total number of years teaching experience in general and in their area of specialization. The teachers were asked to identify whether they had participated in any drug education coursework/seminar since that may have occurred outside of their academic training. It also inquired about their perceptions of self-adequacy and training in relation to working with students with special needs. These two questions provided information on how much background knowledge and experience the subject held about drugs and their toxicity, as well as the their perspective of their own ability to work with drug exposed children as a result of that knowledge.

INSTRUMENT DEVELOPMENT

Phase I

The Teacher's Attitude Toward Drug Related Births Scale is an ordered scale constructed after the Thurstonian Model, which permits the application of parametric and nonparametric statistics. The nature of this scale presents a number of previously ranked items, which occupy specific positions (favorable through unfavorable) on the scale. The item statements are strictly opinion statements to which the subjects only responds if they agree with the statement. The subject's description of how they feel about the construct is evaluated based upon their response selection. (Henderson, 1978; Miller, 1991).

The original version of this instrument was constructed and piloted in 1993 with a sample of 80 students. The frequency of the distribution was leptokurtic around the lower end which indicated that there were too many favorable responses. It had a Cronbach's Alpha of .65 after 5 items were eliminated.

Phase II

The current 20 item Thurstonian instrument (Appendix C and D) has been piloted with 21 teachers from the Boston area. To construct the instrument, a revised pool of 54 opinion statements were compiled, incorporating a spectrum of eleven evaluative opinions from favorable, neutral, to unfavorable, with additional unfavorable items. Favorability values were obtained by soliciting 20 judges, to sort the 54 scale statements according to the eleven categories. The evaluation of the responses was solely based on the favorableness or unfavorableness of the items. A factor analysis was employed and three judges were eliminated due to consistently extreme responses. Ambiguous items with a large response variability (> 2.7 standard deviation) were excluded from the scale. Twenty items were then selected and randomly printed on a form with instructions. The respondent's scale score consists of the mean values of all of the items with which there is agreement (Mueller, 1986).

Pilot Study

The pilot study was conducted to determine if teachers experienced difficulty with the wording of the scale items. The study was conducted with public school teachers (n=21) in the Boston area. The convenience sample consisted of both regular and special education teachers who are currently teaching in the Boston area public schools, most of whom volunteered through graduate courses at a local college.

Standard statistics were conducted on the data from the pilot study of twenty-one cases. Three items had zero variance due to either complete agreement by the respondents with the item, or complete disagreement by the respondents. The reliability analysis (Cronbachs alpha) indicated an alpha of .75 for the other seventeen items to which there was 100% response. The total mean for the scale was 7.4 and standard deviation was 2.4. The factor analysis produced three latent factors; 1) those who relate with and are concerned about these children; 2) those who advocate for the educational rights of these children; and 3) those who have some animosity due to the social impact of their presence. Essentially these results indicate that there were responses in each of the three categories of favorable, neutral and unfavorable.

DESCRIPTION OF THE INSTRUMENTS

All subjects completed the Attitude Toward Children of Drug Related Births Inventory (Hubbard, 1994), the Marlowe-Crowne Social Desirability Scale and a general demographic form (See Appendix D and E). The attitudinal object is children of drug related births, that is children who had some level of chemicals, specifically crack/cocaine in their system at birth. The Thurstonian model was chosen because of the existence of a "zero" or neutral point. This allows for absolute interpretation of scale scores rather than only relative interpretation (in which scores have meaning only relative to the scores of other respondents). An attitude score at the neutral point on a Thurstone scale can truly be interpreted as a neutral attitude (Mueller, 1986, p.44). The final instrument contains 20 items with scale values that range from 2 to 10, with favorable items registered as the lower scale values (See Table 3.2). The subjects were directed to indicate a response by marking whether they agreed or disagreed with a given statement. One point was scored for each item with which the respondent agreed. The median score was used as the attitude indicator.

Table 3.2: Item Summary of ATDB Scale

Scale Items	Item Value
C1. Children of substance abusers are everyone's concern.	9
C2. Children of substance abusers are filling up the public schools.	10
C3. Children of substance abusers should attend special schools.	10
C4. Teachers should know if children of substance abusers are in their classes.	6
C5. I would like to help children of substance abusers.	3
C6. Children of substance abusers should be placed in Special Education classes.	9
C7. Schools need more information about children of substance abusers.	2
C8. Children of substance abusers should not play with other children.	11
C9. The behavior of children of substance abusers is unpredictable.	8
C10. People spend too much time talking about children of substance abusers.	10
C11. Children of substance abusers will need a special classroom environment.	4
C12. Children of substance abusers are too dangerous for public schools.	11
C13. Children of substance abusers have no self-control.	10
C14. No one in the school should know if a student is a child of substance abusers.	7
C15. Children of substance abusers can lead normal lives.	2
C16. Children of substance abusers should be in regular classrooms.	5
C17. Children of substance abusers may be disruptive in class.	10
C18. I know children of substance abusers.	6
C19. Children of substance abusers can not keep up with other children.	10
C20. Children of substance abusers can progress with extra assistance.	4

Note. The higher the number, the more unfavorable the item.

The short form of the Marlowe-Crowne Social Desirability Scale was administered in this study to monitor the degree of socially desirable responses (See Appendix D). This scale was initially developed with the interpretation "that people conform to social stereotypes of what is good to acknowledge concerning oneself in order to achieve approval from others" (Crowne & Marlowe, 1964, p.26).

The scale is a tool for measuring a need for approval, which could confound the interpretation of the results of the Attitude Toward Children of Drug Related Births Inventory. This need for approval varies in people and those with greater need, will engage in culturally sanctioned behavior and thus avoid genuine responses. The short form of the Marlowe-Crowne was used in this study which contains 13 true or false items, and has an overall alpha of .74. The scores on this inventory can range from 1 to 13, with the higher scores indicating a greater degree of socially desirable responses.

The demographic form (Appendix E) was used to elicit typical background information and information on each teachers' educational training and years of experience. It also generated data on teachers' perceptions of their ability to work with special populations and their possible perceived needs for further training.

THREATS TO VALIDITY

This study has three major threats to internal validity: a) selection effects, the differences in the reasons the sample chose their concentration (e.g., special education over regular education and vice versa), b) individual history and the nature of previous drug education (i.e., the breath and depth of coursework versus a two hour seminar), and c) reliability of self-report. The first two threats are influential to the results since the decision to enter the education profession as a teacher of special education indicates a difference in intrinsic motivation or goals and educational process. Once enrolled in a formal academic program, the coursework and learning exposure of Special Education will vary from that of the future regular classroom teacher. There may also be a difference in the nature of available coursework in the area of substance abuse. It is possible that some students will be required to complete full college credits in this area while others may only be provided an opportunity to attend a two hour or two day seminar.

The threat of the reliability of self-report in research is not new (Krathwohl, 1993). Participants in research studies have traditionally been burdened with possibilities of bias in various forms throughout time. It is expected that the research design and data analysis has anticipated and reduced these threats as much as possible.

Threats to external validity include the willingness of the sample to participate (i.e., a self-selected sample) and the focus which was teachers in urban schools. Another concern is the inadequate system of reporting/publicizing prenatal drug abuse which has been inconsistent and biased racially and along social-economic stratas (Edwards, Saylor, & Shifflett, 1992; Jaudes & Ekwo, 1994). Most of the statistics and media reports that are influencing teachers, are about poor minority women who are recipients of social services.

In a study by Chasnoff, Landress, & Barrett, (1990), most of the women reported were receiving public health care because of their limited social economic resources, and the majority of them 67% (n=750) were Black. Comparatively in private health care offices, "black women made up less than 10 percent of the patient population but 55 percent of those reported for substance abuse during pregnancy" (p.1204). These issues must be considered before drawing any generalized conclusions.

DATA ANALYSIS

The primary analysis of this study was conducted to test the following hypothesis:

Teachers with training and experience in special education
will hold more favorable attitudes toward children of
crack/cocaine related births in comparison to teachers without
specific special education training and experience.

This hypothesis focuses on testing the relationship of measured attitudes for special education teachers and regular classroom teachers. A one-tailed test of significance was employed with a significance level of $\mu = .05$.

Data analysis was conducted in a series of steps. First, a frequency distribution of all variables was examined for outliers and data entry errors. Second, a reliability analyses was conducted using Cronbach's alpha on the Attitude Toward Children of Drug Related Births Inventory. Only those items contributing to an overall alpha value of .7 or above were used in further analyses. Reliability statistics were also conducted on the Marlowe Crowne.

Correlational analyses were performed to determine; a) the relation of the measured teachers' attitudes and their scores on the Marlowe-Crowne Social Desirability Scale and b) the measured teachers' attitudes and their years of experience teaching. It was determined that if either or both of these correlations were significant, then the significant independent variables (i.e., years of experience, Social Desirability Scale score) were to be used as covariates in the final analyses.

Next, Analysis of Variance (ANOVA or ANCOVA) procedures were used to determine if there are differences in the attitudes of the two groups of teachers. In addition with a suitable distribution in the number of teachers who have (and have not) take a drug education course, a two-way ANOVA was employed. This was with teachers' specialization (special education or regular education) and drug education experience (yes/no) as the two independent variables and teacher attitudes as the outcome.

A chi-square was conducted to examine the discreet data on; 1) the relationship between teacher specialization and prior participation in drug education coursework; 2) the relationship between drug education coursework and self-adequacy; and 3) the relationship between years of experience and self-adequacy.

CHAPTER IV

Findings

This chapter will present the results of the study beginning with the analysis of statistics for the Marlowe-Crowne Social Desirability Scale (MC). The MC was administered to investigate the propensity of socially acceptable responses. It will be followed with the results of the Teachers' Attitude Toward Drug Related Births Inventory (ATDB) which is the core instrument for the study. All procedures were completed using the SPSS program for statistical data analysis and an alpha level of .05 was used for all statistical tests.

THE MARLOWE-CROWNE SCALE

The Marlowe-Crowne Social Desirability Scale is designed to measure the incidence of respondents that are inclined to give responses that they believe are socially acceptable. Table 4.2 illustrates the overall low frequency of teacher responses on socially desirable items. The items with the highest frequencies are items; p4 "There have been times when I felt like rebelling against people in authority even though I knew they were right"; and p8 "I sometimes try to get even rather than forgive and forget." While these items had a high frequency, no item secured 50% or more of the teachers' responses.

The thirteen item, short form of the Marlowe-Crowne had a mean score of μ=4.38 (s=3.35) out of a possible score of 13 points. On this scale, one point is scored for each socially desirable response. The low 4.38 mean score of the Marlowe-Crowne indicates that the sample population did not have an inclination to give socially desirable responses overall. Of the thirteen subjects with a score of zero on the Marlowe-Crowne, 4 of the subjects were special education teachers and 9 were non-special education teachers (see Table 4.3).

A two-way Analysis of Variance (ANOVA) was conducted to determine if scores in the MC varied by type of specialty (i.e., special education or non-special education) or by level of education (i.e., graduate or undergraduate degrees). This analysis produced a main effect for level of education but not for area of specialty and no significant interactions (see Table 4.4). Teachers with graduate degrees had significantly higher scores on the MC in comparison to those with undergraduate degrees, indicating a tendency to give more socially desirable responses (see Table 4.2 and Figure 4.1)

In Table 4.4, ANOVA results indicated that teachers did not vary significantly in terms of their scores on the MC based on their area of specialty (e.g., special education or regular education). The mean scores of both groups are strong indicators that the teachers did not give what they thought were socially acceptable answers (see Table 4.4).

Table 4.1: Group Characteristics By Specialty

| Characteristics | Groups | | | |
	Special Education		Non-Special Education	
Gender	*n*	*%*	*n*	*%*
Male	5	17	24	83
Female	50	36	72	64
Ethnic Group				
Caucasian	28	34	55	66
Non-Caucasian	17	29	41	71
Level of Education				
Undergraduate	20	25	60	75
Graduate	25	41	36	59
Years Teaching				
1-4	13	32	28	68
5-10	12	28	31	72
11+	20	35	37	65

Note. $X^2(1, N = 141) = 3.61, p > .05$ for gender; $X^2(1, N = 141) = .30, p > .05$ for ethnicity; $X^2(1, N = 141) = 4.06, p < .05$ for level of education; $X^2(3, N = 141) = 6.71, p > .05$ for years of teaching experience.

Table 4.2: Frequency Of Marlowe-Crowne Responses

	SCALE ITEM	% TRUE	% FALSE
P1.	It is sometimes hard for me to go on with my work if I am not encouraged.	61.7	38.3*
P2.	I sometimes feel resentful when I don't get my way.	64.5	35.5*
P3.	On a few occasions, I have given up doing something because I thought too little of my ability.	65.2	34.8*
P4.	There have been times when I felt like rebelling against people in authority even though I knew they were right.	56.7	43.3*
P5.	No matter who I'm talking to, I'm always a good listener.	32.6*	67.4
P6.	There have been occasions when I took advantage of someone.	72.3	27.7*
P7.	I'm always willing to admit it when I make a mistake.	34.8*	65.2
P8.	I sometimes try to get even, rather than forgive and forget.	51.1	48.9*
P9.	I am always courteous, even to people who are disagreeable.	38.3*	61.7
P10.	I have never been irked when people expressed ideas very different from my own.	14.9*	85.1
P11.	There have been times when I was quite jealous of the good fortune of others.	68.1	31.9*
P12.	I am sometimes irritated by people who ask favors of me.	70.2	29.8*
P13.	I have never deliberately said something that hurt someone's feelings.	27.7*	72.3

Note. * Socially desirable responses.
Thirteen subjects scored zero on this scale.

Figure 4.1: Cell Means On the Marlowe-Crowne by Education and Specialty

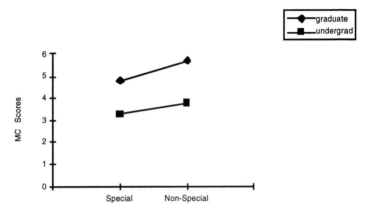

Note. Undergraduate Special Educators n=80; Non-Special n=60.
Graduate Special Educators n=25; Non-Special n=36

Table 4.4 shows that although socially desirable responses did not appear to vary in this sample by type of specialty, they did vary by level of education. As a conservative approach to analysis of the central hypothesis of this study, it was determined that the scores on the MC were to be used as a covariate. This would help determine if the independent variables are confounded by the relationship between attitudes and specialty or attitudes and educational level.

Table 4.3: Mean Scores on the Marlowe-Crowne

Group	n	M	SD
Special Educators	45	4.11	3.40
Non-special Educators	96	4.51	3.33
Total Population	141	4.38	3.35

Note. Maximum score = 13

Table 4.4: Analysis of Variance on the Marlowe-Crowne by Education and Specialty

Source	df	MS	F
Education Level (EL)	1	110.15	10.35*
Specialty (SP)	1	15.69	1.47
EL X SP	1	1.25	.10
Within Groups	137	10.63	
Total	140	11.23	

Note. *p<.05

PRELIMINARY ANALYSIS ON THE ATDB

The ATDB is designed to measure teachers' attitudes toward children of drug-related births. The twenty item scale had a reliability coefficient of .8409.

As indicated in Table 4.5, the frequency results of the scale's item responses indicated a wide range of agreement. Ten of the twenty items had over 50% of the respondents agree with the statement, and eight of those ten items had an agreement frequency of 70% or better. Content of items with a high frequency of agreement include items about a concern and a need for more information aboutdrug-exposed children (c7, c1); a desire to help these children (c5); and an expectation of behavior problems (c17). Conversely, only 7.8% (n=11) of the teachers agreed with item c8, which states that "Children of substance abusers should not play with other children". Another high disagreement item (n=14) is c14, which states that, "No one in the school should know if a student is a child of substance abusers".

The ATDB scales were scored using an assigned value for each item ranging from 2.5 to 10. The higher mean scores on this scale indicate greater levels of unfavorable attitudes toward drug-exposed children, while lower scores are an indicator of more favorable attitudes. Only those responses to which the respondent indicated agreement contributed to the overall score. The sample population (N=141) scored a scale mean of μ=2.95 (s=1.17) based upon those items with which they agreed.

Table 4.5: Item Summary of ATDB Scale

Scale Items	% Agree	% Disagree
C1. Children of substance abusers are everyone's concern.	87.9	12.1
C2. Children of substance abusers are filling up the public schools.	59.6	40.4
C3. Children of substance abusers should attend special schools.	19.1	80.9
C4. Teachers should know if children of substance abusers are in their classes.	72.3	27.7
C5. I would like to help children of substance abusers.	84.4	15.6
C6. Children of substance abusers should be placed in Special Education classes.	30.5	69.5
C7. Schools need more information about children of substance abusers.	98.6	1.4
C8. Children of substance abusers should not play with other children.	7.8	92.2
C9. The behavior of children of substance abusers is unpredictable.	48.9	51.1
C10. People spend too much time talking about children of substance abusers.	22.7	77.3
C11. Children of substance abusers will need a special classroom environment.	44.0	56.0
C12. Children of substance abusers are too dangerous for public schools.	14.2	85.8
C13. Children of substance abusers have no self-control.	29.8	70.2
C14. No one in the school should know if a student is a child of substance abusers.	9.9	90.1
C15. Children of substance abusers can lead normal lives.	74.5	25.5
C16. Children of substance abusers should be in regular classrooms.	70.2	29.8
C17. Children of substance abusers may be disruptive in class.	84.4	15.6
C18. I know children of substance abusers.	65.2	34.8
C19. Children of substance abusers can not keep up with other children.	34.0	66.0
C20. Children of substance abusers can progress with extra assistance.	74.5	25.5

FACTOR ANALYSIS

A factor analysis was used on the ATDB to examine the factor structure of the scale. DeVellis (1991) reiterates the role of the "elbow" in a scree plot, and the importance of the factors that explain a substantial amount of the variance, versus those factors that evolve below the elbow and explain relatively little (Robinson, Shaver & Wrightsman, 1991). The factor analysis scree test revealed only one meaningful factor (see Figure 4.2), for which DeVellis (1991) refers to Cattell's guidelines for recommending the rejection of those factors below this elbow.

Factor analysis also examined the top two factors. The first factor involved School Related Attitudes and Personal Attitudes (see Table 4.6) which has an eigenvalue of 5.42, and constitutes 27 percent of the variance. The items that create this factor, are items that demonstrate school related attitudes based upon the expected behavior of the drug-exposed child within the educational environment.

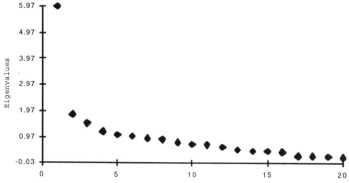

Figure 4.2: Scree plot points represent a distinct elbow supporting the interpretation using one factor.

The second much smaller factor (3 items) has an eigenvalue of 1.10, which accounts for 5.5 percent of the variance. These items discuss knowledge issues of the needs and rights of the school, the teacher, and the student. The two factors together account for a 32.7 cumulative percentage. The factor output represented in Table 4.7 shows a low factor correlation of .05.

Tests of reliability were performed on the twenty item ATDB scale and the top two subscales. The twenty item scale produced a

Cronbach's a = .84; the seventeen item scale produced a Cronbach's a=.86; while the three item scale from the second factor has a Cronbach's a=.23. Given the similarities in the reliability on the 17 item and 20 item scale, and the low reliability on the 3 item scale, this study reports the findings on the ATDB as one twenty item scale with one factor.

Table 4.6: Summary of Items for Factors 1 and 2

Item	Description
	Factor 1—School Related Attitudes
1. c15R	Children of substance abusers can lead normal lives.
2. c12	Children of substance abusers are too dangerous for public schools.
3. c13	Children of substance abusers have no self- control.
4. c16R	Children of substance abusers should be in regular classrooms.
5. c19	Children of substance abusers can not keep up with other children.
6. c8	Children of substance abusers should not play with other children.
7. c5R	Schools need more information about children of substance abusers.
8. c3	Children of substance abusers should attend special schools.
9. c6	Children of substance abusers should be placed in Special Education classes.
10. c10	People spend too much time talking about children of substance abusers.
11. c20R	Children of substance abusers can progress with extra assistance.
12. c11	Children of substance abusers will need a special classroom environment.
13. c9	The behavior of children of substance abusers is unpredictable.
14. c1R	Children of substance abusers are everyone's concern.
15. c2	Children of substance abusers are filling up the public schools.
16. c17	Children of substance abusers may be disruptive in class.
17. c18R	I know children of substance abusers.
	Factor 2—Personal Attitudes
1. c4	Teachers should know if children of substance abusers are in their classes.
2. c7R	Schools need more information about children of substance abusers.
3. c14R	No one in the school should know if a student is a child of substance abusers.

Table 4.7: Partial Output of Factor Analysis

Factor Correlation Matrix	Factor 1	Factor 2
Factor 1	1.0000	
Factor 2	.0500	1.0000

ANALYSIS OF THE CENTRAL HYPOTHESIS

Teachers with training and experience in special education, will hold more favorable attitudes toward children of crack/cocaine related births, in comparison to teachers without specific special education training and experience.

The Teachers' Attitude Toward Drug-Related Births Inventory (ATDB) has a negative and non-significant correlation with the Marlowe-Crowne Social Desirability Scale ($r = -.14$; $p > .05$). This correlation indicates that the low scores on the ATDB, which indicate favorable attitudes, were not associated significantly with high scores on the Marlowe-Crowne, which would have indicated that these were more socially desirable responses. Because of the direction of the correlation and the significant difference found on the MC for teachers with different levels of education, the analysis of the hypothesis was conducted both with and without the MC as a covariate. As the results did not vary, analyses are presented here using the most conservative approach (i.e., including the MC as a covariate). The ANOVA comparing special educators with non-special educators on the Teachers' Attitude Toward Drug Related Births Inventory (ATDB) resulted in a range of means scores (m =2.94 to m=6.15), which illustrated favorable to neutral attitudes overall (s=1.17).

Descriptive statistics for the two samples, special education teachers and non-special education teachers, on the Teachers' Attitude Toward Drug Related Births Inventory (ATDB), are reported in Table 4.8. Higher mean scores on this scale indicate more unfavorable attitudes toward children with drug-related births (see Table 4.8). Non-special educators, as a group, held higher mean scores but also a higher standard deviation.

Table 4.8: Mean Scores of Special Education and Non-Special Education Teachers on the ATDB Inventory.

Group	*M*	*SD*	*n*
Special Ed.	2.56	.887	45
Non-Special Ed.	3.13	1.250	96

The hypothesis was analyzed using a two-way analysis of covariance (ANCOVA), with the scores on the Marlowe-Crowne as the covariate.

The results of the Teachers' Attitude Toward Drug Related Births Inventory (Hubbard, 1994) support the hypothesis that there is a difference between the Special Education teachers and the Non-special Education teachers. The lower mean scores indicate that Special Education teachers hold a more positive attitude than the regular classroom teachers toward the drug-exposed children.

Because of the educational disparity in the two groups, the results were further analyzed by group membership (special education and non-special education) and level of education (graduate degree and undergraduate degree). As displayed in Table 4.9 and Figure 4.3, the results indicate a main effect for specialty area, no main effect for level of education but a significant interaction effect. In both educational groups the special education teachers' scores were lower (see Table 4.10).

This interaction suggests that the overall results must be considered in the context of a significant interaction effect. The most favorable attitudes were held by special educators with an undergraduate degree, and the least favorable attitudes were held by non-special education undergraduate level teachers.

Table 4.9: Analysis of Variance On the ATDB by Education and Specialty With the Marlowe-Crowne as Covariate.

Source	*df*	MS	ATDB
Marlowe-Crowne	1	3.84	3.03
Specialty (SP)	1	8.95	7.06*
Education Level (EL)	1	1.34	1.06
EL X SP	1	4.95	3.91*
Within group	*136*	*1.26*	
Total	140	1.38	

Note. *p<.05

A further examination of the data indicated that the Marlowe-Crowne was not a significant source of variation (p>.05) despite its relation to education levels. This would support that the demonstrated difference between the ATDB scores reflecting the teachers' attitudes overall, was not confounded by socially desirable responses (see Table 4.9).

Figure 4.3: A Comparison of Mean ATDB Scores For Teachers by Education and Specialty

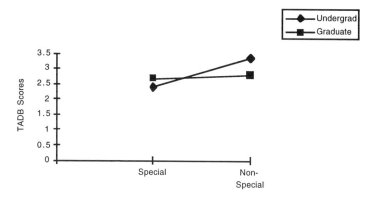

Note. Special Education undergraduates n=20; graduates n=25
Non-special Education undergraduates n=60; graduates n=36

Table 4.10: Mean Scores of Special Education and Non-Special Education Teachers on the ATDB Inventory by Education Level.

Group	M	n
Special Ed.		
Graduate	2.68	25
Undergraduate	2.41	20
Non-Special Ed.		
Graduate	2.78	36
Undergraduate	3.34	60

Note. This interaction of specialty and educational level was significant at $p < .05$

ANALYSIS OF ALTERNATIVE EXPLANATIONS FOR RESULTS

Additional analyses were conducted to examine alternative explanations of the results. Three specific alternative explanations for the results of this study could be tested using data from this sample:

1) Results varied by years of teaching experience;
2) Results varied by participation in drug education courses; and
3) Results varied by belief in having received adequate training to work with children with special needs.

The sample ($N = 141$), was asked to respond with either "yes" or "no" to the question, "Have you ever participated in a Drug Education course/seminar?" The sample had a proportion of teachers (29%) who reported that they have had previous drug education coursework (n=40). Of the special education teachers, 37% (n = 17), indicated that they had previous coursework in the area of drug education. Among the regular classroom teachers (n = 96), 24% (n=23) reported prior drug education coursework. Using chi-square analysis, it was found that more special educators had participated in such a course $X^2(1, N = 141) = 2.87$, $p = .08$. An ANCOVA was conducted to determine if participation in a drug education course was associated with more favorable (i.e., lower) scores on the ATDB. The ANOVA findings in Table 4.11 show no significant effect of drug education nor of interaction between specialty and drug education. These results neutralize the argument that the more favorable attitude of the special education teachers, was a result of prior drug education coursework by the special education teachers.

Table 4.11: Analysis of Variance of ATDB Scores by Drug Education and Teacher Specialty

| Source | df | ATDB SCORES | |
		MS	F
Drug Education (DE)	1	2.58	1.99
Specialty (SP)	1	8.39	6.46*
DE X SP	1	2.90	.137
Within Groups	137	1.29	
Total	140	1.38	

Note. *p<.05

The chi-square procedure examined the association between the teachers' specialty and their beliefs about their ability to work with special needs children. The teachers were asked to respond to the question, "Do you feel adequately trained to work with children with special needs in your classroom?" In contrasting the special education teachers and the regular classroom teachers, 75% of the special education teachers (n=45) reported that they believed they were adequately trained to work with special needs children, while only 15% of the regular classroom teachers (n=96), reported similar perceptions. The relationship between special education backgrounds and beliefs of self-adequacy in working with special needs children are significant $X^2(1, N = 141) = 48.53, p < .05$. These special education teachers demonstrate more positive attitudes toward the drug-exposed population.

A similar chi-square evaluation of the number of years of teaching experience and the teachers' self-adequacy revealed that regardless of the number of years of teaching experience, only 34% of the teachers feel competent in working with children with special needs $X^2(3, N = 141) = 12.49, p <.05$.

An ANOVA was conducted on the ATDB by teachers' years of teaching experience and specialty (special education and non-special education). The four categories included; new teachers; those with 1-4 years of experience; 5-10 years of experience; and 11 or more years of experience. Table 4.12 presents an analysis of variance on the ATDB, and teachers' years of experience revealed no significant findings (p>.05). While the effects by specialty again revealed a significant difference (p<.05).

Table 4.12: Analysis of Variance of ATDB Scores by Teaching Experience and Teacher Specialty

		ATDB SCORES	
Source	*df*	*MS*	*F*
Teaching Experience (TE)	3	.465	.343
Specialty (SP)	1	10.59	7.819*
TE X SP	3	.528	.390
Within Groups	*133*	*1.355*	
Total	140	1.380	

Note. *p<.05

Table 4.13: Percentage of Item Agreement by Teachers on the ATDB Scale

Scale Items		Special Ed.	Non-Special
C1.	Children of substance abusers are everyone's concern.	93.3	85.4
C2.	Children of substance abusers are filling up the public schools.	55.6	61.5
C3.	Children of substance abusers should attend special schools.	13.3	21.9
C4.	Teachers should know if children of substance abusers are in their classes.	68.9	74.0
C5.	I would like to help children of substance abusers.	95.6	79.2
C6.	Children of substance abusers should be placed in Special Education classes.	31.1	30.2
C7.	Schools need more information about children of substance abusers.	100.0	97.9
C8.	Children of substance abusers should not play with other children.	0.0	11.5
C9.	The behavior of children of substance abusers is unpredictable.	40.0	53.1
C10.	People spend too much time talking about children of substance abusers.	4.4	31.3
C11.	Children of substance abusers will need a special classroom environment.	48.9	41.7
C12.	Children of substance abusers are too dangerous for public schools.	2.2	19.8
C13.	Children of substance abusers have no self-control.	11.1	38.5
C14.	No one in the school should know if a student is a child of substance abusers.	4.4	12.7
C15.	Children of substance abusers can lead normal lives.	84.9	67.7
C16.	Children of substance abusers should be in regular classrooms.	77.8	66.7
C17.	Children of substance abusers may be disruptive in class.	80.0	86.5
C18.	know children of substance abusers.	71.1	62.5
C19.	Children of substance abusers can not keep up with other children.	17.8	41.7
C20.	Children of substance abusers can progress with extra assistance.	91.1	66.7

CHAPTER V

Discussion

The target population of this study (n=141) included two groups of teachers, those with special education background and those classified as regular classroom teachers. Respondents held either undergraduate or graduate level degrees, and they were a diverse group representing the New England area. Results indicated that those teachers who held favorable attitudes toward children of drug-related births held many of the feelings of inadequacy and concerns about helping these children as did others with a less favorable attitude.

SUMMARY

The basis for this study revolves around teachers' attitudes toward drug-exposed children by exploring issues of teacher expectations, years of teaching experience and preservice training. The influence of environmental factors on an individual's values and belief system are pivotal in the development of attitudes. This study explores the interactions between the teachers' value systems, their training, their perceptions of drug-exposed children, and their expectations of drug-exposed children. These attitudes are derived from a myriad of sources including the media and other avenues of accurate and misinformation and shared misconceptions. To that effect it is important to note that almost 100% of the sample agreed with item c7, "Schools need more information about children of substance abusers."

This inquiry into teachers' attitude was initiated by using the Attitudes Toward Drug-Related Births (Hubbard, 1994), a paper and pencil self-report questionnaire. The instrument was designed to elicit a response of either agree or disagree to specific items relating to drug-exposed children.

The challenge of securing a non-biased response from teachers to a construct such as an attitude toward children is formidable. To account for the possibility of this confounder, the Marlowe-Crowne Social Desirability Scale was included as part of this study. The results of this measure strengthen the outcomes of the ATDB by demonstrating that the attitude instrument outcomes were not an attempt by the subjects to be perceived in a socially acceptable manner. The findings from this scale indicate a low inclination by both groups to generate socially desirable responses. The non-special education teachers did have slightly higher scores which would indicate a greater desire to be socially accepted, however the difference between the two groups was not significant. While the scores on the ATDB support the hypothesis, the Marlowe-Crowne scores diminish the possibility that the more favorable attitudes of the special education teachers, is influenced by the desire of this group to give socially desirable responses.

This investigation into the attitudes of teachers toward drug-related births supported the projected hypothesis that:

Teachers with training and experience in special education, will hold more favorable attitudes toward children of crack/cocaine related births, in comparison to teachers without specific special education training and experience.

This hypothesis addresses the question of whether there is a difference in attitudes toward drug-exposed children in Special Education and Non-special education educators. Even with 32 percent of the sample certified in Special Education, it is interesting to note that the mean score for both groups on the ATDB fell within the favorable to neutral ranges. This inquiry into teachers' attitudes indicates a less than favorable attitude toward drug-exposed children overall, and yet it does not support a particularly strong unfavorable attitude. The highest scores on the ATDB for both groups were at the less favorable end of the neutral range or 6.15 out of 11.

The possible role of the years of teaching experience, prompted an examination into the number of years of teaching experience and its possible influence on teachers' attitudes. Teachers' attitudes toward the drug-exposed population could stem from the number of years that a teacher has been in the field, and that could have had an effect on the scale responses in either direction (i.e., the more teaching experience one has the more or less favorable one's attitude becomes). The study found that the number of years of teaching experience did not have a significant relation to the samples' attitudes of participants in this study.

Another question revolves around the issue of drug education coursework. Would having prior drug-education coursework make a difference in whether teachers generate a favorable or unfavorable response/attitude toward drug-exposed children? Do the special education teachers' have more drug education coursework in their backgrounds? An exploration around how the subjects perceive their ability to work with special-needs students and their concerns about how well informed they are about these children, may relate to their involvement in some preservice or other drug curriculums. This finding is based upon the teachers' responses to item number B9 on the demographics survey, "Have you ever participated in a Drug Education course/seminar?" Seventy-one percent responded that they have had no drug education coursework. It is difficult to draw any specific conclusions from the responses to this item, because there is no indication of the depth or breath of any of the coursework the participants may have taken. A positive response to this item could range from a teacher participating in an one hour seminar, to a course or degree/certification program.

This then leads to the third question for investigation, which is whether there is something specific about the training in a Special Education teacher's background that promotes a more favorable attitude toward drug-exposed children. It is the author's belief that the preservice training that special education teachers receive generates a more favorable attitude, which goes beyond the self-selection into the specialization.

An exploration of whether the special education teachers' training and experience had an influential role in the differences between the groups, reveals some complex findings that support the hypothesis. For the special education teachers, 75 percent of the 45 teachers responded that they felt adequately trained to work with this population, compared with 16 percent of the 96 non-special education teachers who so responded that they feel adequately trained. The results of two other chi-squares that examine self-adequacy items, are consistent across both groups in that the years of teaching experience, did not create a positive belief in the teacher's ability to work with special needs children. These results are consistent with the findings by Chapman & Elliott (1995) in a survey of a group of Headstart teachers. Eighty-six percent of these teachers (n=72) indicated that one of their "most significant concerns" was "a lack of course work related to children exposed to cocaine/illicit substances" and, "A lack of practicum or supervised hands-on-experiences with this population." (Chapman & Elliott, 1995, p. 124).

Another finding about special education teachers' training, that supports the argument that it is something in their training as a specialist that manifests as a more favorable attitude, is the finding that only 37 percent of this group has had a specific drug education course or seminar. Nonetheless, the special education teachers have developed a more favorable attitude towards drug exposed children.

An unexpected finding was that almost half (43 percent) of the teachers with graduate degrees felt adequately trained to work with special needs children. Those with graduate degrees make up two-thirds of the group that do feel adequate in working with special needs children. However, this group's scores were at the midway point on the Marlowe-Crowne, which means teachers with graduate degrees were found to respond in a significantly more socially desirable manner than those teachers with only undergraduate degrees.

Meaning of the Findings

The high agreement with item c1. " Children of substance abusers are everyone's concern." and the moderate agreement by the non-special education teachers with item c7. "I would like to help children of substance abusers", helps to illustrate the challenge drug-exposed children face (see Table 4.13). The belief that there is a concern for drug-exposed children but not as much desire to help them supports the findings of Siegel & Moore (1994). The 46 teachers in that study were found to have unfavorable attitudes toward special education students when compared to non-special education students, but the teachers held higher levels of concern for those same special needs students.

Most of the teachers agree that teachers should know if there is a drug-exposed child in their classroom, and yet only 67% of the non-special education teachers agree that these children can progress with extra assistance, or that they can lead normal lives. This perspective contradicts the research, that does not support a specific developmental profile of drug-exposed children (Chasnoff, 1992) and could border on perpetuating the myths generated by the media.

There are two items; c8 "Children of substance abusers should not play with other children" and c12 "Children of substance abusers have no self-control"; with scale values of 11, which is the most unfavorable attitude score possible on this scale. Eleven of the non-special education (n=96) teachers agreed with item c8 "Children of substance abusers should not play with other children", and none of the special education teachers (n=45) agreed with the item. Nineteen non-special education teachers and one special education teacher agreed with item c12, "Children of substance abusers are too dangerous for public schools." While these numbers are low, they support the argument that members of the teaching population do harbor unfavorable attitudes toward drug-exposed children, however they are in the minority.

Agreement responses to another item c4. "Teachers should know if children of substance abusers are in their classes", shows that over 50% of the teachers in both groups feel that they should know if a drug-exposed child is in their classroom. This knowledge could be helpful to both the child and the teacher if it is not going to result in less favorable attitudes and subsequently less favorable expectations and treatment of these children. If teachers are given the information on drug-exposed children that they have indicated they need, it could alleviate the heightened concerns that teachers may have developed over time.

LIMITATIONS OF THE STUDY

One of the limitations of the study is that both groups of teachers studied are from the early/elementary education levels. The attitudes of teachers who work with older age groups of students may differ. Therefore the generalizability of the study results, may be restricted to those educators who work with children at an early/elementary school level.

Another concern may be that all of the participants were from the New England area, and that the sample was a volunteer group. However, there was no compensation given for the subject's participation.

Conclusions

The study supports the hypothesis: Teachers with training and experience in special education will hold more favorable attitudes toward children of crack/cocaine related births, in comparison to teachers without specific special education training and experience, and explores the subtle differences between the two sample groups. It has examined the misconceptions that are often borne in the media and the impact those misconceptions may have on teachers' attitudes and the future of our youth.

The atypicalities in development and behavior emphasized in the research literature suggests consequential concerns for the parenting, education and socialization of drug-exposed children. As these children mature, successful integration into the school system requires careful consideration.

The teachers in the study have clearly indicated a desire for more information about drug-exposed children. They have also revealed their perceptions and concerns about their own inadequacies to work with drug-exposed children.

The training that special education teachers receive may make a difference in their attitudes toward drug-exposed children. Nevertheless many special education teachers indicated that they need more information before they will feel adequate in their capacity to work with drug-exposed children.

Based upon reliability coefficients, the ATDB demonstrated that it is an appropriate instrument for the investigation of attitudes. The coupling of the ATDB with the Marlowe-Crowne also provided assurance that the results minimized bias toward socially desirable responses.

PRACTICAL IMPLICATIONS

Without any specific physiological profile, identification of drug-exposed children is a difficult task (Miller, 1992; Snodgrass, 1994). Cocaine-exposed children have a wide range of physical appearances and abilities. Those teachers who are experienced and trained to identify and implement intervention strategies for children with special needs, may have difficulty recognizing and meeting the needs of some of the drug-exposed children. Some goals that have traditionally been acceptable for special needs students, such as increased eye contact, may have to be reevaluated as a goal for drug-exposed children (NASDES, 1992).

Those children with early prenatal and perinatal difficulties that created neurological disabilities, may be more easily noticed, particularly if their prenatal insults resulted in retardation. Symptoms of decreased attention span, receptive and expressive language delays, disorganization, depressed problem-solving abilities, a limited capacity to persist at difficult tasks, and poor self-regulation may be inconsistently present in varying degrees, and can have great implications for the classroom teacher (NASDSE, 1992).

The main implication is that training and increased awareness can have an impact. Because of this belief that training has an impact the following includes some of the information teachers should know about working with the drug-exposed population.

Some of the drug-exposed children are underidentified because they may be overly compliant, particularly since they are not able to make choices and initiate. They often do not display any physical indications of drug-exposure, and most will not be easily recognized as such. The signal that there is some developmental delay may not manifest itself until the classroom teacher notes a detached, or conversely overactive, behavior. As with all children, teachers should expect an array of behaviors and strengths and limitations (NASDSE, 1992). The drug-exposed child may not interact well with their peers in that they may be aggressive or hyperactive, or they may appear withdrawn and uninterested in social interactions (Kantrowitz, et al, 1990, National Association State Directors of Special Education, Inc., 1992). This difficulty in play may influence their opportunities for social interactions with peers, which is very important in child development (Kantrowitz, et al, 1990). The difficulty of children of drug related births to form emotional attachments and to generate emotional responses does not easily go away, and this difficulty is considered to be a contributor to the poor prognosis of later educational adaptation (Rist, 1990). Researchers (Hofkosh, et al., 1995) have found that interventions of support services for the mother may generate more positive outcomes for the exposed child.

Drug exposed children may be self-absorbed and impulsive, and are slower in understanding cause and effect relationships. Much of their play is random and unfocused, and throughout their educational path they may continue to have problems with executive functions of planning. Older children have shown violent tendencies, an aversion to eye contact with others, and they often display socially unacceptable behaviors such as lying and stealing (Howe & Howe, 1989; Waller, 1993).

There are a variety of developmental disabilities and behavioral disorders that drug-exposed children may display. While any child may find themselves in a frustrating educational situation from time to time, the tolerance level of children exposed to cocaine appears to have a lower level. Sensory stimulation for these children can often be easily overwhelming throughout their early years and the results may be frustrating to the unsuspecting classroom teacher as well (Rist, 1990).

Poor spatial relations in basic perceptual-motor skills like pencil use, block play and shoe tying are to be expected (Poulsen, 1992).

This unpredictable behavior profile may create a caveat for working with behavior modifications. When approaching behavior as a function of the environment, the inconsistent feedback from their interactions with others, can make the progression along a socially acceptable behavior continuum a target of resistance. Unaddressed, this possible resistance could be a subsequent deterrent to maximizing their intellectual and developmental potential (Rist, 1990).

The aberrant behavior of the drug-exposed child may be accompanied by an inability to concentrate and complete information processing, poor fine-motor skills and an inability to follow directions (Gregorchik, 1992; Howe & Howe, 1989; Van Dyke & Fox, 1990). Other difficulties may include the testing of limits set by adults, difficulty in reading social cues, sporadic mastery of skills, auditory processing and word retrieval difficulties (Vincent, 1991).

Increasing opportunities for individualized instruction will be helpful. This may require some intense goal setting and scaffolding by the teacher or a competent peer (Byrnes, 1996). Teaching one shape at a time, songs without accompaniment or just a humming activity may work towards not overloading the child (Waller, 1993).

Schools could also benefit these children by providing an adult-child ratio that promotes nurturing and the development of coping mechanisms. Issues around classroom management and classroom climate need to be reevaluated by teachers and administrators. Traditional classroom orientations may not be adequate for drug-exposed children, consequently, social skills and play will also need to be taught, through "direct-instruction in sharing, greeting, and thanking (p.59)."

Kinesthetic stimulation should be used in moderation with drug-exposed children since many will be easily overstimulated by touch. Waller (1993) suggests that a teacher may place a child's hand on a particular page for emphasis, but be aware that touching, speaking and looking directly at the child may be overwhelming. The use of a low voice while touching the child and avoiding eye contact may be a more successful technique.

A reorganization of the classroom decor so that materials and decorations are removed or kept to a minimal to reduce stimuli until they are appropriate. A proactive approach is the establishment of a highly structured complimentary classroom climate, which includes daily routines and small group instruction. It may be necessary to constantly monitor task completion for these children, due to the lack of perseverance (Waller, 1993).

Teachers working with drug-exposed children should make a conscious effort to modify transitions between activities in such a manner that these children can easily assimilate themselves into the next activity. This would specifically include movement from active to quiet activity, hallway movements like lunch, and other classes or dismissal (Rist, 1990; Waller, 1993). The transition itself should be considered an activity within and of itself, which will benefit the child's ability to deal with change. Encouraging parental involvement in similar routines and structures at home may help with the development of self-regulation, particularly in a unconventional home environments where drug abuse and neglect is continuing.

Since attachment issues are difficult for these children, slow attachment processes should be implemented, along with prolonged involvement with one teacher, which may help facilitate a trusting relationship. This may require that the drug-exposed child be given extra attention and nurturing in order to facilitate their learning experiences. It may also require that specific learning strategies may need to be overemphasized for these children, particularly metamemory strategies and metacognitive functions.

Levels of intervention by the classroom teacher can be primary, secondary or tertiary. Many schools are actively involved in primary and secondary interventions through drug prevention programs and an interdisciplinary approach to referrals for social services. The engagement in capacity building activities for the children to optimize their learning potential and school performance is a tertiary approach (Phi Delta Kappan, 1992).

Teachers' approach toward drug-exposed children should emphasize long-term expectations through simple, unimodal experiences. These activities may need to focus on verbal language development rather than non-verbal cues (facial expressions) which may be misinterpreted (Waller, 1993). Poulsen (1992, p.49) suggest some of the following among a list of strategies:

self-esteem
- provide for adult-child interactions
- provide the children with toys of their own for the day
- encourage the re-creation of daily living experiences through representational play
- encourage and praise all attempts at developmental mastery

behavior
- review daily routines
- match behavioral expectations with behavioral maturity
- build in relaxation as part of the program
- provide a self-selected plan of respite for instances of feeling overwhelmed

disorganized behavior
- develop an appreciation for cause effects of behavior
- guide peer interactions (turn taking)
- allow practice of developmental tasks with a tolerance for messiness

Acceptance of drug-exposed children and a focus on de-labeling, since we do not need another category for labeling children are starting points for policy-makers and administrators. Prenatal cocaine-exposure knows no boundaries of socio-economic position or ethnic background. There should not be an expectation that this is a poor urban problem, since suburban mothers are often more able to hide their substance abuse during pregnancy, and thus the camouflage the initial impact on fetal development (Krajicek, 1992). Consequently many drug-exposed children may never be identified (Waller, 1993).

Teachers need to secure support networks for themselves and the parents of these children to ameliorate negative attitudes toward the child. Increased training of parents, professionals and paraprofessionals in observing and reading behavioral cues will help with intervention. Close attention to drug-exposed children's methods of experiencing stress, coping skills, and reactions to change can provide insight to their behavior (Krajicek, 1992; Lumsden, 1990). It can also help to promote a strong school-home relationship.

It is also important for interdisciplinary teams to "have a basic knowledge of child development and the special problems associated with high-risk children" (Gregorchik, 1992, p.708). This increased knowledge can increase tolerance and patience.

There is hope that through the development of educational programs for teachers about the needs and problems of drug-exposed children, that all teachers will be able to attend to the needs of these children in the regular classroom environment (Lumsden, 1990).

RECOMMENDATIONS FOR FURTHER RESEARCH

The author recommends that further research should be conducted to evaluate the attitudes of teachers at the middle school and high school levels. It would be beneficial to conduct an nationwide survey of urban and rural districts to determine the baseline of teachers attitudes toward drug-related births that could fuel the implementation of training as an intervention.

Future studies should distinguish between the types of drug education coursework taken to better determine what inservice treatment would best serve the needs of the teachers. A clarification should also be made to determine if there is a distinction being made between teachers self-efficacy and feeling adequately trained. These attempts should also involve the preservice teachers that are transitioning into school systems, since items c_1, c_5 and c_7, in Table 4.5 show a high percentage of teachers desiring more information. These results also support a continued infusion of drug-education for teachers, administrators and policy makers is needed to help create a positive environment in which drug-exposed children may learn.

Appendices

APPENDIX A

Dear Teachers,

Enclosed you will find a short questionnaire for my dissertation project, that has just recently been approved by the Boston School Committee. As a teacher myself, I realize this is an extremely busy time of the year, but I sincerely need your assistance. Please take a few minutes to read the enclosed materials and complete the survey. I will pick up the packet from the office in a few days, and will share the results with you in the fall.

Thank you very much!
Lady June Hubbard

APPENDIX B

Sample Research Participation Consent Form

"Children of Drug Related Births"

You are being invited to participate in a research study, designed to investigate the attitudes of teachers, toward children who had drugs in their system at birth. You are being invited on the basis of your teaching career, and your educational background. The purpose of the study is to examine the range of attitudes toward these children, and the degree to which various factors may influence those attitudes. The information gained from this study may assist various educational personnel in designing and implementing educational programs and staff development.

Your participation in this study would be greatly appreciated, however you do not have to participate if you do not wish. You may also withdraw from the study at any time. You will be asked to anonymously complete a questionnaire that relates to the topic, and to provide some background information. All data from this study will be compiled and analyzed in such a way that only summary results will be given: no single individual will be identifiable. All information from the questionnaire is confidential.

It is the researcher's belief that this study may be a beneficial exercise to the participant's growth as well, and you are encouraged to contact her to discuss this study. If you wish to discuss any aspect of this study, you may call: Lady June Hubbard, (617) 868-0249, or write to PO Box 381143 Cambridge, MA 02238.

APPENDIX C

Sample Instruction Page

Dear Participant,
Thank you for agreeing to complete this survey. Please rest assured that your responses are confidential and unidentifiable. Some sections of the questionnaire may seem unconventional, but they are important to the study. Therefore, I would like to take this opportunity to request that you please respond to **each item**, so that the best possible statistical results can be obtained.

Sincerely,

Lady June Hubbard

APPENDIX D

Children of Substance Abusers (COSA)

For the purpose of this inventory, Children/Child of Substance Abusers (COSA), are those children who had some level of chemicals, specifically crack/cocaine, in their system at birth. Try to indicate either agreement or disagreement for each statement. This is not an examination. There are no right or wrong answers to these statements.

Please indicate your own convictions by circling "**A**" when you **Agree** at some level with an item, and circling "**D**" when you **Disagree**. **Please respond to each item.**

A D C1. Children of substance abusers are everyone's concern.

A D C2. Children of substance abusers are filling up the public schools.

A D C3. Children of substance abusers should attend special schools.

A D C4. Teachers should know if children of substance abusers are in their classes.

A D C5. I would like to help children of substance abusers.

A D C6. Children of substance abusers should be placed in Special Education classes.

A D C7. Schools need more information about children of substance abusers.

A D C8. Children of substance abuser should not play with other children.

A D C9. The behavior of children of substance abusers is unpredictable.

A D C10. People spend too much time talking about children of substance abusers.

A D C11. Children of substance abusers will need a special classroom environment.

A D C12. Children of substance abusers are too dangerous for public schools.

A D C13. Children of substance abusers have no self-control.

A D C14. No one in the school should know if a student is a child of substance abusers.

A D C15. Children of substance abusers can lead normal lives.

A D C16. Children of substance abusers should be in regular classrooms.

A D C17. Children of substance abusers may be disruptive in class.

A D C18. I know children of substance abusers.

A D C19. Children of substance abusers can not keep up with other children.

A D C20. Children of substance abusers can progress with extra assistance.

APPENDIX E

Personal Reaction Inventory

Listed below are a number of statements concerning personal attitudes and traits. Read each item and decide whether the statement is **true** or **false** as it pertains to you personally. Please circle "**T**" for **true** or "**F**" for **false**.

T F P1. It is sometimes hard for me to go on with my work if I am not encouraged.

T F P2. I sometimes feel resentful when I don't get my way.

T F P3. On a few occasions, I have given up doing something because I thought too little of my ability.

T F P4. There have been times when I felt like rebelling against people in authority even though I knew they were right.

T F P5. No matter who I'm talking to, I'm always a good listener.

T F P6. There have been occasions when I took advantage of someone.

T F P7. I'm always willing to admit it when I make a mistake.

T F P8. I sometimes try to get even, rather than forgive and forget.

T F P9. I am always courteous, even to people who are disagreeable.

T F P10. I have never been irked when people expressed ideas very different from my own.

T F P11. There have been times when I was quite jealous of the good fortune of others.

T F P12. I am sometimes irritated by people who ask favors of me.

T F P13. I have never deliberately said something that hurt someone's feelings.

APPENDIX F

Background Information

Please circle or fill-in the blank for the most appropriate answer.
Please **respond to each item.**

B1. Gender:　　Female　　Male

B2. ____Age

B3. Ethnicity:　Caucasian　African-American　Native American
　　　　　　　Hispanic　　Caribbean　　　　African
　　　　　　　Asian　　　Other

B4. Educational Level:
　1) Undergraduate degree
　2) Graduate degree(s)

B5. Teacher Training:
　1) Early/Elementary
　2) Middle
　3) Secondary
　4) Not relevant

B6. Teaching Experience:
　1) new
　2) 1-4 yrs
　3) 5-10 yrs
　4) 11+ yrs.
　5) None

B7. Specialization:
　1) Special Ed.
　2) Reading
　3)Counseling
　4) Math/Science
　5) Other
　6) Not relevant

B8. Years Experience in Specialization:
　1) new
　2) 1-5 yrs
　3) 6-10 yrs

4) 11+ yrs.
5) Not relevant

B9. Have you ever participated in a Drug Education course/seminar?
Yes   No

B10. Do you feel adequately trained to work with children with special needs in your classroom?   Yes   No

Thank you for participating in this survey. Please check to make sure you have responded to each item.

References

Alessandri, S., Sullivan, M., Wolman, M., Imaizumi, S., & Lewis, M. (1993). Learning and emotional responsivity in cocaine-exposed infants. *Developmental Psychology, 29*, 989-997.

Barton, S. J., Harrigan, R., Tse, A.M. (1995). Prenatal cocaine exposure: Implications for practice, policy development, and needs for future research. *Journal of Perinatology, 15*(1), 10-22.

Bellisimo, Y. (1990, Jan.). Crack babies: The schools' new high-risk students. *Thrust*, 23-26. (ERIC Document Reproduction Service No. ED 338443)

Bogardus, E. (1931). *Introduction to sociology* (5th ed). Los Angeles: Jesse Ray Miller.

Bronfenbrenner, U. (1979). *The Ecology of Human Development*. Iowa: W.C. Brown Publishers.

Bronfenbrenner, U. (1986). Ecology of the family as a context for human development: research perspectives. *Developmental Psychology, 22*(6), 723-742.

Burnison, J. (1991). Testimony as executive director of NAPRE [summary]. Testimony on Drug Exposed Children: Effective Intervention (pp. 17-21). U.S. House of Representatives Select Committee on Narcotics Abuse and Control.

Byrnes, J.P. (1996). *Cognitive Development and Learning in Instructional Contexts*. Boston: Allyn and Bacon.

Center for Early Education and Development (1990). Children of Cocaine: facing the issues. *Fact Find*. (Eric Document Reproduction Service ED 320358).

Chapman J.K., Elliot, R. (1995). Preschoolers exposed to cocaine: Early childhood special education and head start preparation. *Journal of Early Intervention, 19*(2), 118-129.

Chasnoff, I. J. (1992, August). Cocaine, pregnancy, and the growing child. *Current Problems in Pediatrics*, 302-321.

Chasnoff, I. J., Griffith, D. R., MacGregor, S., Dirkes, K., & Burns, K. A. (1989). Temporal patterns of cocaine use in pregnancy. *Journal of the American Medical Association, 261*(12), 1741-1744.

Chasnoff, I. J., Griffith, D., Freier, C., & Murray, J. (1992). Cocaine/polydrug use in pregnancy: two-year follow-up. *Pediatrics, 89*(2), 284-290.

Chasnoff, I. (1989). Cocaine, pregnancy, and the neonate. *Women & Health, 15*(3), 23-34.

Chasnoff, I., Landress, H., & Barrett, M. (1990). The prevalence of illicit-drug or alcohol use during pregnancy and discrepancies in mandatory reporting in Pinellas County Florida. *The New England Journal of Medicine, 322*(17), 1202-1206.

Cole, M., & Cole, S. (1993) *The development of children*. California: Scientific American Books.

Colmorgen, G. (1988). Drug screening in prenatal care demands objective medical criteria, support services. *Journal of the American Medical Association, 264*(3), 309-310.

Crowne, D. & Marlowe, D. (1964). *The approval motive: studies in evaluative dependence*. New York: Wiley & Sons.

Davis, E. (1991). Report on drug-related births at Harlem hospital [summary]. Testimony on Drug Exposed Children Effective Intervention (pp. 41-45). U.S. House of Representatives Select Committee on Narcotics Abuse and Control.

Davis, E., Fennoy, I., Kanem, N., Brown, G. & Mitchell, J. (1992). Autism and developmental abnormalities in children with perinatal cocaine exposure. *Journal of the National Medical Association, 84*(4), 315-319.

Deoliveira, I. J., & Cratty, B. J. (1991). Survey of ten infants exposed prenatally to maternal cocaine use. *International Journal of Rehabilitation Research, 14*, 265-266.

DeVellis, R.F. (1991). *Scale Development: theory and applications*. London: Sage Publications.

Dixon, S., Bresnahan, K., & Zuckerman, B. (1990, June). Cocaine babies: meeting the challenge of management. *Contemporary Pediatrics*, 70-92.

Dotts, W. (1978). Black and white teacher attitude toward the disadvantaged and poverty. *Education, 99*, 48-54.

Dusek, J. & Joseph, G. (1983). The bases of teacher expectancies: a meta-analysis. *Journal of Educational Psychology, 75*(3), 327-346.

Dusick, A., Covert, R., Schreiber, M., Yee, G., Moore, C. & Tebbett, I. (1993). Risk of intracranial hemorrhage and other adverse outcomes after cocaine exposure in a cohort of 323 very low birth weight infants. *Journal of Pediatrics, 122*, 438-445.

Eagly, A., & Chaiken, S. (1993). *The psychology of attitudes.* Fort Worth: Harcourt Brace Jovanovich, Inc.

Edwards, I, Saylor, & Shifflett, B. (1992). Drug exposed infants in the social welfare system and juvenile court. *Child Abuse & Neglect, 19*(1), 83-91.

Frank, D. , & Zuckerman, B. (1993). Children exposed to cocaine prenatally: pieces of the puzzle. Neurotoxicology and Teratology, 15, 298-300.

Elliott, K. & Coker, D. (199?). Crack babies: Here they come, ready or not. *Journal of Instructional Psychology, 18*(1), 60-64.

Gingras, J. L., Weese-Mayer, D. E., Hume, R., & O'Donnell, K. J. (1992). Cocaine and development: mechanism of fetal toxicity and neonatal consequences of prenatal cocaine exposure. *Early Human Development, 31*, 1-24.

Gold, M. (1993). *Cocaine.* Plenum Medical Book Company: New York.

Gonzalez, N. & Campbell, M. (1994). Cocaine babies: Does prenatal exposure to cocaine affect development? *Journal of the American Academy of Child Adolescent Psychiatry, 33*(1), 16-27.

Greer, J. (1990). The drug babies. *Exceptional Children, 56*(5), 382-384.

Gregorchik, L. (1992). The cocaine-exposed children are here. *Phi Delta Kappan*, 709-711.

Griffith, D., Azuma, S., & Chasnoff, I. (1994). Three-year outcome of children exposed prenatally to drugs. *Journal of the American Academy of Child Adolescent Psychiatry, 33*(1), 20-27.

Hawley, T. & Disney, E. (1992). Crack's children: the consequences of maternal cocaine abuse. *Society for Research in Child Development. Social Policy Report, 6*(4), 1-20.

Henerson, M.E., Morris, L.L., & Fitz-Gibbon, C.T. (1978). How to measure attitudes. Sage Publications: Beverly Hills.

Hofkosh, D., Pringle, J., Wald, H., Switala, J., Hinderliter, S., & Hamel, S. (1995). *Archives of Pediatric-Adolescent Medicine, 149*, 665-672.

Howard, B.J., & O'Donnell, K. (1995). What is important about a study of within-group differences of 'cocaine babies'? *Archives of Pediatric-Adolescent Medicine, 149*, 663-664.

Howard, J. (1991). *Developmental outcome of children exposed prenatally to drugs.* Los Angeles: University of California, Los Angeles, Department of Pediatrics.

Howe, K, & Howe, W. (1989). Children of Cocaine: treatment and child care. Factsheets presented at the Annual Conference of the National Association for the Education of Young Children. Atlanta, GA, November, 2-5, 1989.

Hurt, H., Brodsky, N.L., Betancourt, L., Braitman, L.E., Malmud, E.,
    Giannetta, J. (1995), *Developmental and Behavioral Pediatrics, 16*(1), 29-
    35.

Jacques, J. & Snyder, N. (1991). Newborn victims of addiction. *Registered
    Nurse*, 47-52.

Jaudes, P. & Ekwo, E. (1994). Association of drug abuse and child abuse. *Child
    Abuse & Neglect, 19*(9), 1065-1075.

Jones, M. (1991). An endangered generation: Impact of perinatal drug use.
    Paper presented at the Annual Student Services Statewide Conference,
    Winston-Salem, NC.

Kaye, K., Elkind, L., Goldberg, D., & Tytun, A. (1989). Birth outcomes for
    infants of drug abusing mothers. New York *State Journal of Medicine, 89*,
    256-261.

Krajicek, M. (1992). Interventions for infants born affected by drugs and
    alcohol. In Bunsen, T., (Ed.) Forum on Emerging Trends in Special
    Education: Implications for Personnnel Preparation. (4th Washington,
    D.C., April 9-10, 1992: see EC 301793).

Kronstadt, D. (Spring 1991). Complex developmental issues of prenatal drug
    exposure. *The Future of Children*, 1-14.

Leavitt, F. (1995). Drugs and behavior. California: Sage Publications.

Lester, B., Corwin, M. J., Sepkoski, C., Seifer, R., Peucker, M., McLaughlin,
    S., & Golub, H.L. (1991). Neurobehavioral syndromes in cocaine-exposed
    newborn infants. *Child Development, 62*, 694-705.

Lewin, K. (1935). *The dynamic theory of personality*. New York: McGraw-
    Hill.

Lewis, M., Bendersky, M.(Eds.) (1995). *Mothers, babies and cocaine*. New
    Jersey: Lawrence Erlbaum Associates, Publishers.

Lumsden, L. (1990). Meeting the special needs of drug-affected children. Eric
    Digest Series. (ERIC Document Reproduction Service No. ED231424).

Miller, S. (1992). Policy options: Early intervention services for substance-
    exposed infants. *Journal of Drug Education, 22*(4), 273-281.

Mueller, D. (1986). *Measuring social attitudes*. New York: Teachers College
    Press.

National Association of State Directors of Special Education, Inc.(1992).
    Children Exposed in Utero to Illegal drugs: Education's newest crisis.
    Liaison Bulletin: 18(2), Jan.

National Health/Education Consortium (1991). Healthy brain development: a
    precursor to learning. (ERIC Document Reproduction Service No ED).

National Health/Education Consortium (1992). Cocaine-Exposed Children: A Growing Health/Education Issue. (ERIC Document Reproduction Service No ED 355037).

National Institutes of Health (1996). National Pregnancy & Health Survey. NIH Publication No. 96-3819.

Nieto, S. (1992). *Affirming diversity: the sociopolitical context of multicultural education.* New York: Longman Publishing Group.

Office of National Drug Control Policy (Spr.1996). Pulse Check: National Trends in Drug Abuse.

Richardson, G., Day, N. (1994). Detrimental effects of prenatal cocaine exposure: Illusion or reality? *Journal of the American Academy of Child & Adolescent Psychiatry, 33*(1), 28-34.

Richardson, G., &Day, N. (1996). Prenatal cocaine exposure: effects on the development of school-age children. *Neurotoxicology and Teratology,* 6(6), 627-634.

Rist, M. (1990, January). The shadow children. *American School Board Journal,* 19-24.

Robinson, J.P., Shaver, P.R., & Wrightsman, L.S.(Eds.) (1991). Measures of Personality and Social Psychological Attitudes. San Diego: Academic Press, Inc.

Rodning, C., Beckwith, L., & Howard, J. (1989). Characteristics of attachment organization and play organization in prenatally drug-exposed toddlers. *Development and Psychopathology, 1,* 277-289.

Rubovitz, P., Maher, M. (1973). Pygmalion in black and white. *Journal of Personality and Social Psychology, 25*(2), 210-218.

Ryan, L., Ehrlich, S. & Finnegan, L. (1987). Cocaine abuse in pregnancy: Effects on the fetus and newborn. *Neurotoxicology and Teratology, 9,* 295-299.

Sallee, F. R., Katikaneni, L. P., McArthur, P. D., Ibrahim, H. M., Nesbitt, L., Sethuraman, G. (1995). Head growth in cocaine-exposed infants: Relationship to neonate hair level. *Developmental and Behavioral Pediatrics, 16*(2), 77-81.

Snodgrass, R. (1994). Cocaine babies: A result of multiple teratogenic influences. *Journal of Child Neurology, 9*(3), 227-233.

Van Baar, A. (1990). Development of infants of drug dependent mothers. *Journal of Child Psychology, 31*(6), 911-920.

Van Dyke, D., & Fox, A. (1990). Fetal drug exposure and its possible implications for learning in the preschool and school-age population. *Journal of Learning Disabilities, 23*(3), 160-163.

Waller, M. (1993). Helping crack-affected children succeed. *Educational Leadership*, 57-60.

Weiss, R.D., Mirin, S.M., & Bartel, R.L., (1994). *Cocaine*. Washington, DC.: American Psychiatric Press, Inc.

Werner, E. (1994). Overcoming the odds. *Developmental and Behavioral Pediatrics, 15*(2),l31-136.

Weston, D.R., Ivins, B., Zuckerman, B., Jones, C., & Lopez, R.(1989). Drug Exposed Babies: Research and Clinical Issues. *Zero to Three, 9*(5), 1-7.

Woods, N., Eyler, F. D., Behnke, M., & Conlon M. (1990). Cocaine use during pregnancy: maternal depressive symptoms and infant neurobehavior over the first month. *Infant Behavior and Development, 10*, 83-99.

Zuckerman, B., & Frank, D. (1994). Prenatal cocaine exposure:nine years later. *Journal of Pediatrics,* 124, 731-733.

Zuckerman, B., & Frank, D. (1992). Crack Kids: Not Broken. *Pediatrics, 89*(2), 337-339.

Zuckerman, B., Frank, D., Hingson, R., Amaro, H., Levenson, S., Kayne, H., Parker, S., Vinci, R., Aboagye, K., Fried, L., Cabral, H., Timperi, R., & Bauchner, H. (1989). Effects of maternal marijuana and cocaine use on fetal growth. *New England Journal of Medicine, 320*(12), 762-768.

Index